Toagoodman, E.
RocColumna

W9-BVR-578

IN THE MIDST
OF OUR STORMS

IN THE MIDST
OF OUR STORMS

Opening Ourselves to Christ in the Liturgy

ROC O'CONNOR

LTP

LITURGY
TRAINING
PUBLICATIONS

Nihil Obstat
Very Reverend Daniel A. Smilanic, JCD
Vicar for Canonical Services
Archdiocese of Chicago
November 20, 2014

Imprimatur
Most Reverend Francis J. Kane, DD
Vicar General
Archdiocese of Chicago
November 20, 2014

The *Nihil Obstat* and *Imprimatur* are declarations that the material is free from doctrinal or moral error, and thus is granted permission to publish in accordance with c. 827. No legal responsibility is assumed by the grant of this permission. No implication is contained herein that those who have granted the *Nihil Obstat* and *Imprimatur* agree with the content, opinions, or statements expressed.

Scripture quotations are from the *New Revised Standard Version Bible: Catholic Edition*, copyright © 1989, 1993, National Council of Churches of Christ in the United States of America. Used with permission. All rights reserved.

Excerpts from the English translation of *The Roman Missal* © 2010, International Commission on English in the Liturgy Corporation. All rights reserved.

Excerpt from *THE AWFUL ROWING TOWARD GOD* by Anne Sexton. Copyright © 1975 by Loring Conant, Jr., Executor of the Estate of Anne Sexton, renewed 2003 by Linda G. Sexton. Reprinted by permission of Houghton Mifflin Harcourt Publishing Company. All rights reserved.

Reprinted by permission of SLL/Sterling Lord Literistic, Inc. Copyright by Anne Sexton.

"maggie and milly and molly and may". Copyright © 1956, 1984, 1991 by the Trustees for the E. E. Cummings Trust, from *COMPLETE POEMS: 1904–1962* by E. E. Cummings, edited by George Firmage. Used by permission of Liveright Publishing Corporation.

IN THE MIDST OF OUR STORMS: OPENING OURSELVES TO CHRIST IN THE LITURGY © 2015 Archdiocese of Chicago: Liturgy Training Publications, 3949 South Racine Avenue, Chicago, IL, 60609; 1-800-933-1800, fax 1-800-933-7-94, e-mail orders@ltp.org. All rights reserved. See our website at www.LTP.org.

Text © Robert F. O'Connor Jr., SJ

"In the Midst of Our Storms" art © 2014 Renée Malloy Ludlam

Printed in the United States of America

Library of Congress Control Number: 2014950486

19 18 17 16 15   1 2 3 4 5

ISBN: 978-1-61671-236-5

IMOS

To Mom & Dad,

Mary Elizabeth Cotter O'Connor (1926–1989)
and
Robert Fuller O'Connor Sr. (1922–2003),

who gave me enough yet not enough.

Gratefully,
Your Son

In distress you called,
and I rescued you;
I answered you
in the secret place
of thunder.

(Psalm 81:7)

CONTENTS

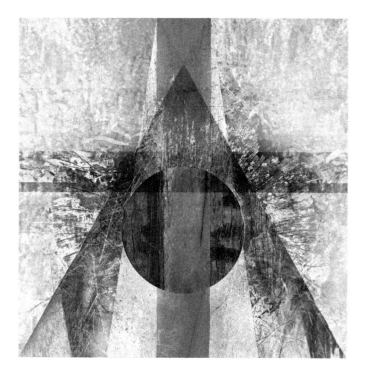

PREFACE

I started writing this book in January 2004, four months after Dad died and fifteen years after Mom died. Little did I realize how even more significant and beloved their influence would become. The blessings and limitations of family, Catholic education in the 1950s and '60s, and Jesuit formation from the latter part of the twentieth century provided me enough ambition, knowledge, denial, compassion, self-centeredness, and hope to become a lifelong learner.

I have planned, played, and led liturgical music at Mass from the spring of 1968 even until the publication of this book. Sometime after almost thirty years of music ministry, I had to admit I was bored. A decade or more of loss and disillusionment left me little connection with what was sung, preached, proclaimed, or ritualized. It had all become routine, and I knew I needed to search for meaning and understanding. Even still, I could not yet account for the breadth of my alienation from God, self, and others. I was left piloting a boatload of questions on a stormy sea.

A robust foundation for my sense of liturgical prayer had been established in league with John Foley, SJ, Bob Dufford, SJ,

Dan Schutte, and Tim Manion, the St. Louis Jesuits. Nevertheless, new questions required deeper seeking. I asked, "How can anyone praise God after betrayal?" and "Why do I resist the Word of God so strongly?"

Along the way I questioned friends. Rick Dalby, Kathy Lewis, and Bob and Kate Boland took me seriously enough to engage in hearty discussions at early conventions of the National Association of Pastoral Musicians. There, I would ask: Why does what we do at Mass not feel like worship? What *is* liturgical prayer? Their willingness to talk about important liturgical matters kept me asking questions and seeking answers.

Many in the congregations I served all through these years resonated with such questions. I salute the parishioners of the former Immaculate Heart of Mary Parish and the Sunday night Catholic Mass community at Macalester College in St. Paul, Minnesota (1993–99); the staff and parishioners at the Church of the Gesu, Milwaukee (1985–88); St. Luke's Church, St. Paul (1988–91); St. Ann's Church, Boston, Massachusetts (1991–93); Holy Trinity Parish, Washington, DC (1999–2000); the Jesuit Community and St. John's Parish at Creighton University, Omaha, Nebraska (2000–2013); and St. Francis Xavier College Church, St. Louis, Missouri (2013–14).

In 1991, I returned to school, first at the former Weston School of Theology (1991–93), where I met my friend, Paula Cuozzo, who has been a consistent, insightful, and supportive interlocutor for many years. At Weston, our friend and mentor, Peter Fink, sj, opened the personalist dimension of liturgical relationships in a seminar on the philosophy of John Macmurray. I also acknowledge my professors at The Catholic University of America (1999–2000), Msgr. Kevin Irwin, Margaret Mary Kelleher, osu, and David Power, omi, whose love of God and liturgy opened my mind and heart to the mystery at the heart of liturgy. At Catholic U., I converted to liturgy as "the act of Christ and of the Church" (*General Instruction of the Roman Missal*, 19).

During those years of study, I learned a lot and welcomed new ideas and insights that helped me pray at liturgy. Yet, something was missing. It was while on sabbatical (2013–14) that the significance of St. Ignatius of Loyola's emphasis on conversion of the affections (emotions) came home to me. I knew a bunch. I just didn't know how to let it in personally. This other conversion gave me more tools to live these ideals with fewer pretenses. For that gift, I thank my many new friends in St. Louis whose commitment to exploring personal depths has been inspiring. You confirmed in me the importance of leading from my weakness. You showed me ways to dwell in divine serenity. God bless all of you!

Many thanks to Samara Rafert (and her husband, Dan Gearino), who took on the role of first editor and helped me better understand the process of writing. I'm grateful to Anne

Osdieck and Tim Grosch, who not only read various drafts of this project but also provided intelligent and perceptive feedback during the latter months of my editing. I recognize Trish Sullivan Vanni, who saw value in this book project, gave it a transformative edit, and submitted it to Liturgy Training Publications (LTP). I am indebted to John A. Thomas, director at LTP, for taking a chance on this manuscript. Thank you each so much.

Finally, I am grateful to my editor at LTP, Mary G. Fox, who introduced me to the world of book publishing and who put the final touches on the text. I'm grateful for her professionalism, her competence, and her gracious humanity that has made the completion of this project a joy.

—Roc O'Connor, SJ
Church of the Gesu
Milwaukee, Wisconsin
September 7, 2014

Introduction

Christ always truly associates the Church with himself in this great work wherein God is perfectly glorified and the recipients made holy. . . . In the liturgy the whole public worship is performed by the Mystical Body of Jesus Christ, that is, by the Head and his members.

Constitution on the Sacred Liturgy, 7

—◄◄◄◄—

The *Constitution on the Sacred Liturgy* (CSL) describes the liturgy as a "great work" (7) that glorifies God and makes the People of God holy. In this act of public worship, the article explains, the Mystical Body of Christ is revealed as one—Head and members. The words of the *Constitution* profoundly spoke to me when I returned to them at the beginning of the twenty-first century. They reshaped my understanding of liturgy as "the act of Christ and of the Church" (*General Instruction of the Roman Missal* [GIRM], 19).

Also adding richness to my understanding of communal prayer was Msgr. Annibale Bugnini's observation, "The liturgy is theology in the form of prayer," in *The Reform of the Liturgy: 1948–1975*. Bugnini's thought not only summed up my newfound delight in the meaning of liturgical prayer but also

> **The Constitution on the Sacred Liturgy (CSL)**, the first document of the Second Vatican Council, provided the theological and pastoral overview and direction for liturgical reforms after the Council.

sharpened my desire to connect liturgical theology and human experience. This book flows directly from that gladness.

I have no solution to any of the conflicts concerning liturgy and liturgical style. What I wish to share instead are insights into, and a method for, connecting liturgical theology with the experience of living worshippers, whatever their liturgical sensibilities.

The questions that will focus our inquiry include: How does liturgy situate worshippers before God? How do theology, liturgy, and liturgical theology address experience? How do Word, gesture, and symbol guide believers into their most vulnerable depths to encounter the Risen Christ anew? How do disciples-in-training journey from where they are to where the liturgy calls us?

The joys and sorrows of my life generated these questions. Personal challenges have fired my desire for a more substantial engagement with Jesus Christ, the Paschal Mystery. This book outlines a spiritual approach to encountering the Real Presence.

I believe in the Real Presence, and I have come to see that my struggle to consciously encounter that Real Presence has not so much to do with God but with myself. I have sought a greater experience of my real presence to God, self, and the world, yet for a host of reasons, that intimacy has eluded me. Fortunately, God has blessed me with companion-seekers along

Liturgy refers to sacramental rites and ritual actions. Among these rites and actions are the rites of Baptism of adults and infants, Confirmation, Anointing of the Sick, the Mass, vigil services before funerals, and Benediction. (Adjectival form: *liturgical*)

Liturgical theology reflects upon both the texts, and the implementation, of liturgy to draw out the underlying theological content.

the way. Since you picked up this book, perhaps you count yourself among such pilgrims. If so, welcome!

Allow me to provide a blueprint for what follows. The book is divided into four parts. We will consider the meaning of the Paschal Mystery, our encounter with the Word of God, our resistance to the Word of God, and the method of Liturgical Contemplative Practice, in which we bring our emotional reactions that keep us from engaging with the Real Presence.

As we study the Paschal Mystery in chapter 1, we will look at the One whom we engage in liturgy, the Risen Christ, as a personal reality. Serving as our guide will be the text from St. Paul's Letter to the Philippians 2:5–11: "Christ . . . emptied himself." It is crucial to grasp the profound dynamism

Liturgical gesture: Consider any hand gesture as a metaphor for ritual elements performed, given, offered, or extended toward the faithful. Any action during the liturgy can be seen as a gesture. Every action, from the Entrance Procession through singing, kneeling, bowing, putting money in the collection, to being sent forth, is a gesture. One of the key gestures in the liturgy is the proclamation of the Word.

Disciples-in-training: I will use this rather inelegant term to underline the ongoing nature of following Christ. We are always students, even as we are sometimes teachers.

Paschal Mystery is an opaque term at best and an impenetrable one at worst. To approach the meaning of this term, think of Christ at the right hand of God. I attempt to clarify the meaning of the Paschal Mystery in chapter 1. Since the term is dense, more than one reading of the chapter would benefit the reader's understanding.

of the Paschal Mystery as we come to know the mystery of Love Outpoured.

Next, I offer a taste of how liturgy itself sets the parameters for the human encounter with the divine. An inquiry into liturgical word and gesture reveals how a sustained encounter with the Risen Christ can free us from alienation and illusion. The path I will describe encourages us to encounter Christ in our vulnerability, exploring inner places that we fear, or about which we are ashamed. It involves plumbing the inner expanses we usually know only by loss, disappointment, betrayal, or disillusionment. Paradoxically, this is the very exploration that can lead us to be really present to the Paschal Mystery.

Throughout *In the Midst of Our Storms*, I advocate that the renewal of liturgy during the past fifty years has just as much to do with the renewal of conscious participation by the Body of Christ (our real presence) as it does with growing our understanding of worship.

Each of the following three trajectories in this book lead to places in our lives that we tend to sidestep:

The first trajectory is that liturgical engagement with the Paschal Mystery involves encountering the kenotic Christ, the one who is wholly Love Outpoured. Engaging Christ threatens what mystics refer to as the "false self" of the disciple-in-training. Engaging Christ provokes aggressively defensive reactions from those parts of our lives caught in illusions of security, tough-minded independence, or human wisdom. As we recognize, name, and

Kenotic: "[Christ] emptied himself, taking the form of a slave" (Philippians, 2:7). The Greek word provides the noun, *kenosis*, and the adjectival form, *kenotic*, denotes the self-emptying of the Second Person of the Trinity. This is Outpouring Love indeed.

bring these facets of our lives into relation with Christ, we become able to pray with fewer pretenses.

Second, liturgical encounters with the Risen Christ (the Paschal Mystery) reveal hungers and thirsts deep in the

General Instruction of the Roman Missal (GIRM): A theological and pastoral guide to the meaning and purpose of each part of the liturgy. The GIRM illustrates, depicts, and portrays the liturgical landscape, the field of encounter for disciples-in-training.

human heart that shape behaviors, attitudes, and actions. Mindful attentiveness during periods of reflection and prayer outside of the Eucharistic liturgy uncovers our errant inclinations and even our sinfulness. We are reminded that we respond to Christ's summons to worship *as we are,* not as we wish to be.

Finally, liturgical encounters with Christ, who speaks to us in Word, who feeds us in Communion, and who kneels to wash our feet, expose overlooked areas of resistance. Personal strategies for defending our vulnerable selves become unmasked.

Many of us know inner turmoil quite well; others enjoy the luxury of denial. I propose that our inmost places of resistance, hungers, thirsts, and defensive reactions are stormy. The psalmist describes these places as secret (Psalm 81:7). They are only secret when left unexplored, unnamed, or concealed. I invite you on a journey to discover Christ with us in the storms and the gift of encountering him in the Eucharist / liturgical prayer.

This book is my attempt to give you what I have gained through the years. As Peter said to the paralytic at the Beautiful Gate near the Temple, "I have no silver or gold, but what I have I give you" (Acts 3:6).

CHAPTER ONE

The Contours of the Paschal Mystery[2]

In him we live, we move and have our being;
In him the Christ, in him the King: Jesus, the Lord.

Though Son, he did not cling to godliness,
but emptied himself, became a slave: Jesus, the Lord.

Jesus! Jesus! Let all creation bend the knee to the Lord!

"Jesus, the Lord"
Jesus, the Lord (80682) © 1981, Robert F. O'Connor, SJ, and OCP,
5536 NE Hassalo, Portland, OR 97213.
All rights reserved. Used with permission.

What is—rather, *who* is the Paschal Mystery? The English term "paschal" emerged from the confluence of Hebrew (*pesach*, "Passover") and Greek (*pascha*, "Passover"), and flowed through Anglo-French, Old Norman, and Latin into the English *paschal*, meaning "Easter." Some scholars point to a supplemental influence from the Greek verb, *paschō* ("to suffer"). These several streams converge to inform today's meaning.

Paschal Mystery is a dense, theological term that appears frequently in our liturgical prayer. It is shorthand for the belief that

Catholics hold that what Jesus Christ accomplished through his suffering, Death, and Resurrection is still being accomplished today in the Liturgy of the Eucharist. We not only recall this truth, we actively engage Truth (Christ) every time we pray the Mass. By engaging the Paschal Mystery, disciples-in-training pass over from fear, alienation, and illusion through the desert of purification to discover resurrected life through recurring encounters with the Risen Christ.

Unless we acclimate our hearts and minds, unless we forge a link between our experience and this oft-impenetrable term, we consign it to a landfill of pointless theological jargon.

An interpretive key that unlocks the riches of the Paschal Mystery can be found in the Christ-centered hymn from St. Paul's Letter to the Philippians:

> Let the same mind be in you that was in Christ Jesus,
>
> who, though he was in the form of God,
>   did not regard equality with God
>   as something to be exploited,
> but emptied himself [*kenosis*],
>   taking the form of a slave,
>   being born in human likeness.
> And being found in human form,
>   he humbled himself
>   and became obedient to the point of death—
>   even death on a cross.
>
> Therefore God also highly exalted him
>   and gave him the name
>   that is above every name,

so that at the name of Jesus
  every knee should bend,
    in heaven and on earth and under the earth,
and every tongue should confess
  that Jesus Christ is Lord,
  to the glory of God the Father.

(Philippians 2:5–11)

We now turn to investigate five facets of the Paschal Mystery. Each has profound implications for Christian identity.

1. The Paschal Mystery is a person, not a thing. Disciples-in-training encounter not *what*—the *event* of Jesus' Death on the Cross 2,000 years ago—but *whom*: Christ in glory *today*. Not *something*, but *someone*. Not a thing, but the Risen Christ seated at the right hand of the Power *today* whom we engage in and through the Church's liturgical action. Robert Taft, sj, summed this up neatly: "Our liturgy does not celebrate a past event, but a present person, who contains forever all he is and was, and all he has done for us."[3] Liturgical encounters with Love Outpoured, then, are personal.

The *Constitution on the Sacred Liturgy* states the ways that the Church meets Christ's personal presence throughout liturgy:

Christ is always present in his Church, especially in its liturgical celebrations. He is present in the sacrifice of the Mass, not only in the person of his minister . . . but especially under the eucharistic elements. . . . He is present in his word, since it is he himself who speaks when the holy Scriptures are read in the Church. He is present, lastly, when the Church prays and sings. (7)

When discussing the Paschal Mystery, then, it is imperative to bear in mind that worshippers encounter the person of the Risen Christ as the One now dynamically pouring himself out at the right hand of the Father and present to us through the Holy Spirit in any liturgical celebration.

2. The Paschal Mystery reveals the breadth of Christ's identity: Popular Catholic piety has concentrated on the Death of Jesus as the central, saving act of God. This concentration is necessary but not sufficient. Remember how St. Paul depicts kenotic love as Incarnation, ministry, suffering, Death, Resurrection, ascension to glory, and return on the last day. Paul's expansive vision, extending from the godhead to Christ's glorious victory at the end time, unveils the breadth of the meaning of the Paschal Mystery.

While Love Outpoured found its most intense expression of divine kenosis in Jesus' Cross and Resurrection *then,* we still engage the Paschal Mystery *today.* The Council Fathers at the Second Vatican Council expressed it this way:

> The liturgy in its turn moves the faithful, filled with "the paschal sacraments," to be "one in holiness"; it prays that "they may hold fast in their lives to what they have grasped by their faith"; the renewal in the Eucharist of the covenant between the Lord and his people draws the faithful into the compelling love of Christ and sets them on fire. From the liturgy, therefore, particularly the eucharist, grace is poured forth upon us as from a fountain; the liturgy is the source for achieving in the most effective way possible human sanctification and God's glorification, the end to which all the other of the Church's activities are directed.

(CSL, 10)

9

3. The Paschal Mystery is an eternal liturgical reality. This leads us to a challenging concept: since there is only one kenosis, that is, one offering, there is only one liturgy. It is a person, the Risen Christ! The ongoing, complete, and eternal Self-Poured-Out *is* Jesus Christ, risen in glory. *Kenosis* is liturgy. Liturgy is *kenosis*. Kenotic Love Outpoured is liturgy *par excellence*.

Let me say this another way. The eternal, self-emptying liturgy that is the Second Person of the Trinity was revealed in history *then* through the Incarnation, life, ministry, suffering, Death, Resurrection, and Ascension of Jesus of Nazareth. Seated *now* at the right hand of the Father, the Risen Christ pours out praise to the One and offers himself, perpetually interceding for our sake. In other words, since the crux of liturgy is Outpouring Love, then Christ is *indeed* the heavenly liturgy. Christ pours himself forth today in his kenotic orientation toward the One in praise and for the world in intercession.[5]

In our earthly liturgy today, we participate in this dynamic relationship. First, all is redeemed in Christ. All creatures are drawn into Christ's eternal kenosis in praise for creation and thanksgiving for redemption. Second, worshippers share today in eternally dynamic Love Outpoured as a foretaste of the final banquet when God will be all in all. The Council Fathers stated: "In the earthly liturgy we take part in a foretaste of that heavenly liturgy celebrated in the holy city of Jerusalem toward which we journey as pilgrims, where Christ is sitting at the right hand of God, a minister of the holies and of the true tabernacle" (CSL, 8).

Since the Paschal Mystery is the liturgy *whom* and *in whom* we celebrate, "Every liturgical celebration . . . is an action of Christ the Priest and of his Body which is the Church" (CSL, 7). And since liturgy is the action of Christ and the Church, all worshippers discover mutuality with Christ by being "really present" to the Real Presence.

4. The Paschal Mystery reveals kenosis as the heart of the Trinity. John's account of the Gospel proclaims Jesus abiding in the Father ("The Father and I are one" [10:30]). Consequently, Jesus Christ, the Paschal Mystery, reveals the inner life of the godhead as the continual outpouring of love between the divine Persons and outwardly for the sake of humanity and all creation. The Trinity is Outpouring Love.

Edward Kilmartin, SJ, one of the great theologians of the twentieth century, explained:

> A comprehensive explanation of the meaning of the liturgy must take the path that leads back to the life work of the Triune God. It must be shown how Christian liturgy in general, and the chief liturgical-sacramental celebrations of the Church, derive from and are ordered to the deepest and proper Mystery of Christian faith: the self-communication of the Triune God in a history of salvation that is the first fruits of the Trinitarian-heavenly liturgy, already in progress since the ascension of Jesus Christ, and the ascension of those who have died in the Lord.[6]

The Father is the wellspring, the source, the font from which divine love streams forth into the world through the Son's

Incarnation by means of the Spirit. This fountain of love overflowed *then* in the life of Jesus of Nazareth, and does so *today* in worshippers' liturgical encounter with the Risen Christ. The Church, as a result, is immersed in Triune Love Outpoured. So, the Spirit gathers the Church and indwells the Body of Christ while worshippers offer praise and thanks to the One, the Source of all with Christ.

5. Liturgy forms kenotic worshippers as servants of the new creation. Each year during the reading of the Epistle at the Easter Vigil, we hear St. Paul affirm this aspect of our faith. He instructs disciples of every generation to take to heart how Christ's *kenosis* (dying and rising) sets the pattern for Christian identity and mission:

> Do you not know that all of us who have been baptized into Christ Jesus were baptized into his death? Therefore we have been buried with him by baptism into death, so that, just as Christ was raised from the dead by the glory of the Father, so we too might walk in newness of life.

(Romans 6:3–4)

In this excerpt from Romans, St. Paul makes it evident that God's plan is to conform us to Christ by transforming us into kenotic love through our *dying and rising with Christ.* This is our identity in Christ. Kenosis orients us in love outpoured to God and to all creation.

The *Constitution on the Sacred Liturgy* echoes St. Paul's assertion that sacraments unite believers intimately with the Paschal

Mystery, forming disciples-in-training to be oriented toward God and to cooperate in the redemption of all creation.

> Thus, for well-disposed members of the faithful, the effect of the liturgy of the sacraments and sacramentals is that almost every event in their lives is made holy by divine grace that flows from the paschal mystery of Christ's passion, death, and resurrection. . . . The liturgy means also that there is hardly any proper use of material things that cannot be directed toward human sanctification and the praise of God. (61)

Thus, when the Church gathers for liturgy, worshippers participate in the eternally graceful response of Trinitarian Outpouring Love. The Paschal Mystery is at heart, then, an ever-expanding relational reality through which the Trinity draws the Church into the divine dance, the dynamic, mutual indwelling of the Persons of the Trinity we call *perichoresis*. That is, this Divine Community—revealed as Love Outpoured in history through Jesus of Nazareth—draws, forms, and transforms worshippers into its self-same reality.

Put simply, liturgy is the privileged means by which God brings the Church into the sacred dance of kenotic love to conform us to Christ. Conscious liturgical participation is the means by which disciples-in-training learn the dance of Trinitarian life. Liturgy instructs us to be graceful dance partners, taught by our God through Christ in the Spirit. We learn the steps of Christ's self-emptying love as we are drawn regularly into the dance of Outpouring Love during liturgy and oriented toward living out this mystery by dying and rising daily. In effect, we rehearse

Outpouring Love through liturgical rituals of dying to the false self and putting on Christ, and thereby realize our kenotic identity and mission in the world.

To sum up, the Paschal Mystery refers to the personal, Outpouring Love (kenosis) of the Second Person of the Trinity revealed in time through Incarnation, life, Death, Resurrection, Ascension, Reign in Glory, and Second Coming. The Paschal Mystery presents Jesus Christ as his disciples' entryway into the liturgical life of the Trinity through Baptism, plunging us into Love Outpoured. The Church encounters the Paschal Mystery through conscious participation in liturgical prayer and discovers both the mystery of her identity and the decisive meaning of all of life. This is evident as the priest celebrant acclaims, "Through him, and with him, and in him, / O God, almighty Father, / in the unity of the Holy Spirit, / all glory and honor is yours, / for ever and ever," and the congregation responds, "Amen!"

CHAPTER TWO

The Real Presence Outpoured

In the previous chapter we explored the Paschal Mystery as Love Outpoured: the kenotic love of the Trinity revealed in Jesus Christ. This insight helps us prepare spiritually and mentally to participate in the life-giving relationship liturgy establishes between the Paschal Mystery and the People of God, the Church. Believing that Christ is really present, active, and engaged in liturgical prayer opens this relationship to us.

Christ is present in the Eucharistic liturgy in four ways: in the people gathered to pray and sing, the priest celebrant, the Word proclaimed, and most especially under the Eucharistic elements, the consecrated bread and wine (CSL, 7). Not only is Christ really present in these four ways, but he calls us to an equally faithful engagement. Many disciples-in-training whom I have known yearn to become more responsive to Christ by developing greater capacity for mindful attention to the divine presence.

Every ritual action of the liturgy invites mindful presence to God, self, and the world. Arriving, signing with baptismal water, standing, singing, making the Sign of the Cross, dialoguing with the priest celebrant, sitting, listening in silence to Word and homily, tithing, moving in procession, professing faith, opening or folding hands, kneeling, and being sent—each one of these liturgical gestures has the capacity to elicit the real presence of the Body of Christ *inasmuch as participants attend consciously to these moments.* Word received and liturgical gestures engaged become vehicles for the conscious human encounter with the Paschal Mystery.

So, what might human engagement with and reception of the Paschal Mystery look like? When the kenotic Christ sends worshippers to confront dying and rising, what might real presence feel like? To answer these questions, we have to delve into the all-too-human, emotional textures that characterize our lives.

Receiving in the Manner of the Receiver

> maggie and milly and molly and may
> went down to the beach (to play one day)
>
> and maggie discovered a shell that sang
> so sweetly she couldn't remember her troubles, and
>
> milly befriended a stranded star
> whose rays five languid fingers were;
>
> and molly was chased by a horrible thing
> which raced sideways while blowing bubbles: and
>
> may came home with a smooth round stone
> as small as a world and as large as alone.
>
> For whatever we lose (like a you or a me)
> it's always ourselves we find in the sea.

"maggie and milly and molly and may"
E. E. Cummings

During my early years in the Society of Jesus, I learned a few useful Latin phrases from several older Jesuits. One of them was often deployed in shorthand: *Quidquid recipitur.* Upon hearing an inscrutable dictum, I'd ask, "What does *that* mean?" The older priest usually volunteered: *Quidquid recipitur per modum recipientis recipitur*, "Whatever is received is received according to the manner of the one receiving."[7] I simply didn't get it.

Some years later, just as I was beginning to realize how crucial it is to account for the reception of the Paschal Mystery, I happened upon an E. E. Cummings poem that surprisingly illuminated that old Latin saying. In Cummings' rather ordinary images, I understood how Maggie, Milly, Molly, and May each met the sea "according to the manner" of their receiving. There is one ocean, but a wide range of responses to it. A light went on.

In the same way we too meet Christ according to the manner of our receiving. There is one Paschal Mystery, but many ways by which we encounter Love Outpoured. If we neglect our experience, the *how* of receiving the Mystery, we remain marooned at the level of theory and Eucharist becomes something we watch. The distance we create by remaining observers contributes to the numbness that many of us experience at Mass.

Given *quidquid recipitur*, we might ask: What would liturgical participation look like if we noticed and included—factored in, as it were—our uncensored affective responses to kenotic love? What if our liturgical participation were truly *conscious*? I contend that when we, as disciples-in-training, *consciously* encounter Love Outpoured, Christ sends us to our depths. There we discover the truth of our identity in Christ. When we account for our emotional responses to the Paschal Mystery—when we embrace the fact that our responses are as many and varied as those of youths finding themselves at the sea—we find ourselves equipped for a more profound, personal, and real presence to the Risen Christ.

Personal encounters with Outpouring Love share several traits. First and foremost, personal engagement with the Paschal Mystery positions us for that which human beings most earnestly seek, the mutual exchange of love. Further, conscious participation in the Paschal Mystery also locates us as worshippers within the intensely human paradoxes of life and death, giving and receiving, independence and dependence, and the like. We see the important tensions that we deal with in life illuminated: power and vulnerability; control and letting go; emptiness and being filled; security and uncertainty; trust, belief, faith, and caution and doubt; pride and humility; individual and communal; career and vocation; what is mine and what is yours; action and contemplation; comfort and challenge; common-sense living and social justice; social life and service; patience and impatience. The list is unending.

Such a list indicates that participation in the Paschal Mystery can be challenging since it has the power to provoke the range of emotions that are part of any profound personal encounter. It is critical, thirdly, to account for all feelings, from attraction to aversion. Yet, this points to a fundamental issue that needs to be addressed here: disciples-in-training are more likely to be comfortable with "pleasant" emotions, so much so that we habitually discount unpleasant feelings.

When we do this, when we give in to avoidance, we quite effectively pronounce any desire to be really present to the Paschal Mystery dead on arrival. Knowledge itself avails us nothing. A change of heart and the bringing of our visceral resistance to God, self, and the world support us as we seek to be really present to the Real Presence.

CHAPTER THREE

The Contours of Our Real Presence to the Word

In chapter 2, we explored how entry into the Paschal Mystery is not only an encounter with the Triune God but can be an opening into the depths of our human nature. The Paschal Mystery brings worshippers into the liturgical, personal, and dynamic Trinitarian reality revealed in Love Outpoured. And, as we are drawn in, the Paschal Mystery more clearly reveals the mystery of our inner lives. Thus, when we encounter divine kenosis, we risk engaging Mystery as a blessing and as a threat.

To explore this, let's consider the experience of meeting the Paschal Mystery in the Word proclaimed. It's easy to see how this can be experienced as a blessing. To be sure, many passages from the Gospel accounts are consoling and strengthening and a welcome gift to world-weary hearts! Christ tells us of God's steadfast love and comforts us with reassurances that this love never abandons us, even as we stray. The Word speaks tenderly to us, soothes our fears, increases our hope, comforts us in our afflictions, heals places darkened by envy, quenches lust, illuminates our vocations, enables us to forgive wrongs, heals deep hurts, and confirms the divine presence in our lives.

We prize the moments when we realize in our depths that the Real Presence is a blessing! We recognize it as such and are drawn to respond to God completely with a "yes" that leaps from our deepest self. We feel liberated from our burdens and free to pour out our lives. At such times, we gratefully praise God, forgive, reconcile, work for justice, go the extra mile, revel in creation, or celebrate the gifts of others. We gladly give our time to serve, our talent to help, or our treasure to assist the Church's care for the poor and oppressed. Indeed, these consolations help conform us to Outpouring Love.

Ironically, though, this very experience of the abundant blessing of the Real Presence in the Word also creates the conditions in which kenotic love can feel like a "threat" to us. When love establishes a safe place for persons to be in relationship, it also makes room for the negative stuff we habitually avoid. Love, even infatuation, creates an unguarded trust so that everything that needs to be integrated and healed can surface. In this way, the Word-as-blessing generates what is needed for our next step in purification. Opened by the Word to the blessing of God, we become anchored by a strong trust in the love of God. This blessing grounds us and allows us to face all the "stuff" we don't want to face. To take this further, I would assert that without a solid, personal underpinning in kenotic love, we will not mature in our spiritual lives.

Notice your honest reactions while we test this claim. When we listen to the Word proclaimed in the liturgy, our hearts are sometimes listless and jaded and our minds filled with distractions. We are barely present to God, much less to anything or anyone else. Essentially, we're so alienated from our experience that the Word cannot engage us—we cannot see how it intersects with our lives, much less transforms them. We're simply bored, which is a nearly perfect defense against the Word.

At other times, we actively resist the Word. Consciously or unconsciously, we balk at being drawn into the rapids of Love Outpoured. Standing on the brink of the divine rushing river that is the life of the Trinity, we freeze. We shrink back from wading in for fear God will swamp us and carry us away. We refuse to dive in, thinking that we might drown or lose control. We do not trust enough to go with the flow, afraid to be borne away into unknown depths or distant reaches. When catching even the slightest glimpse of this power, this potentially transformative engagement with the Trinity through the Word, we stop short, compelled by fears of losing self, relinquishing autonomy, and surrendering power. We cry, "Stop! No further!" And yet it is in these moments that we are really present to the Risen Christ, who will meet us where we are if we have the courage to remain and welcome our resistance. Put simply, the Real Presence of Christ in the Word plants us in the midst of the very human tension between security and insecurity.

Generally speaking, security is a good thing. Feeling safe gives us a sense of well-being. Undaunted by a host of anxieties, secure people are often self-confident and resilient. They are not inclined to develop unhealthy attachments or addictions. Secure people also seem motivated to lead lives of self-donation for the good of others. Simply put, they trust. They seem to be intuitively open to and dependent upon God's graciousness.

Insecurity, however, is ambiguous. It can produce both positive and negative outcomes. For example, insecurity can make us cautious; caution, in turn, can keep us watchful and alert to danger. Caution often fosters prudence and common sense. Yet insecurity can produce preoccupations with self that border on paranoia. Anxiety, uncertainty, and nagging feelings of inferiority and vulnerability may spring from insecurity.

Looking around, we find insecurity masked in a number of ways. The insecure may look for a messiah to rescue them or become fanatics, fashioning idols from religious figures, celebrities, or athletic teams. They may defend their comfort zones, inflating their self-image to ward off anticipated attacks. Feeling empty, the insecure may seek to fill themselves with drugs, alcohol, food, sex, gambling, or shopping.

What are the implications of engaging the Paschal Mystery from within the tension between security and insecurity called forth by the Word proclaimed? The GIRM states, "when the Sacred Scriptures are read in the Church, God himself speaks to his people, and Christ, present in his word, proclaims the Gospel" (29). The Word proclaimed invites engagement. In the following passage from the Letter to the Hebrews, the encounter with the Word is described in exquisitely bold language:

The word of God is living and laboring energetically, sharper beyond every two-edged sword, passing through as far as the division of soul and spirit, of both joints and marrow; and able to judge thoughts and intentions of a heart. And there is no creature hidden before him, but all things are naked and laid open to the eyes of the one with whom is our account.

(4:12–13, my translation)

The Word challenges us, testing our mettle. The Word holds up a mirror, so that when we look in that mirror, we begin to distinguish secret motives concealed in the shadows. We see more clearly what is hidden, and sometimes we become distraught. In the Word, Christ summons us into an unknown and heady future. He presents us with freedom from illusions by drawing before our eyes the ideals of the Reign of God. The Word beckons us beyond our so-called comfort zones to regard with compassion all the broken, including ourselves.

In the Word, Christ exposes our pretense. As the Word speaks prophetically, we see the hypocrisy that infects our worship. Christ lifts the veil on our neglect of the poor. Love Outpoured blesses the meek and oppressed and denounces the proud and rich: the last are now first; the first are last. If we don't find the Word at once comforting and unsettling, we are probably not listening!

Encountering the Word Consciously: First Effort

Does this illustration of engagement I've just drawn up describe your experience? Does the Word always accomplish its purpose in you? Does the Word truly function as a two-edged sword? Does the Word draw you into kenotic love? The following exercise will help uncover how we receive Christ proclaimed according to the mode of our receiving. This exercise requires responding honestly to selections from Matthew's account of the Gospel. Since these are familiar passages, seek to attempt a fresh encounter with them. Pause in the exercise when you need a break.

- Blessed are the poor in spirit, for theirs is the kingdom of heaven (5:3).

- Blessed are the ones mourning; for they shall be comforted (5:4).

- Blessed are you when people reproach you and persecute you and say all evil against you falsely for my sake. Rejoice and be glad (5:11–12).

- Therefore, if you bring your gift to the altar, and there remember that your brother [or sister] has something against you, leave your gift before the altar and go; first be reconciled to your brother [or sister] and then come, offer your gift (5:23–24).

- So, if your right eye causes you to stumble, pluck it out and cast it from you . . . if your right hand causes you to stumble, cut it off and cast it from you (5:29–30).

- But I tell you, do not oppose evil. But whoever strikes you on the right cheek, turn to him also the other (5:39).

- But I tell you, love your enemies and pray for those persecuting you so that you may be children of your Father in heaven (5:44–45).

- Take heed: do not do your righteousness before others with a view to being seen by them; otherwise you have no reward with your Father in heaven (6:1).

- Do not lay up treasure for yourselves on earth, where moth and rust remove and where thieves dig through and steal, but store up treasures for yourself in heaven (6:19–20).

- Do not suppose that I came to bring peace on the earth; I came not to bring peace, but a sword. For I came to make a person hostile against his father and a daughter against her mother (10:34–35).

- If anyone wishes to come after me, let him/her deny him/herself and take up his/her cross and follow me. For whoever wishes to save his/her life will lose it and whoever loses his/her life for my sake will find it (16:24–25).

- If you wish to be complete, go sell your belongings, and give to the poor, and you will have treasure in heaven; then come, follow me. But, hearing this word, the young man went away grieving, for he had many possessions (19:21–22).

(All of the above are my translations.)

How did you like what you heard? What do you want to say to Jesus? What are your uncensored responses? (We recognize where we are by recording our reactions.) Might they resemble any of the following?

- "Jesus, can we talk? Look, I'm a good person. I go to church regularly. I haven't killed anybody. Isn't that enough?"

- "These are nice ideals, but you just can't live like that in the real world. It's completely wacko to think otherwise!"

- "You talking to me?"

- "I feel so guilty when I hear . . ."

- "I believe, Lord, help my unbelief . . ."

- "I'd really like to live like that, but you're asking way too much. I'm no saint!"

- "Can we talk later, Jesus, after I get my act together? Leave your number. I'll get back to you, OK?"

- "Go away!"

What did the Word provoke in you? Did the Word leave you "naked and laid open to the eyes of the One with whom is our account"? Were you tempted to deflect, explain away, or use some ploy to domesticate the Word, rendering it bland and lifeless? Were you tempted to dull the blade? Were you tempted to defend yourself by aggressively pushing Christ away? In other words, did the Word work?

This first step is easy. The responses that surface when we bring ourselves fully to the moment and stand within the tension between security and insecurity are noted clearly. Secondly, to maintain precision, verbal reactions are translated into feeling statements. The individual begins by saying, "I feel" and fills in the response or emotion, whether that is "annoyed," "hostile," "defensive," "irritated," "anxious," "upset," "rattled," "defiant," "ashamed," "uneasy," "ambivalent," "remorseful," or any of a number of feelings. Why develop this skill for naming the emotion that is associated with a reading? *Because naming our emotional reactions helps identify the very places where the Word pierced us so that we can realize where we need to welcome Christ.*

So, for example, in reaction to the passage from Matthew 5:39 ("Do not oppose evil. But whoever strikes you on the right cheek, turn to him also the other") a disciple-in-training could say, "I feel defiant, defensive, and angry at being told to be so incredibly vulnerable. Go away!" That's just fine. An honest accounting is better than getting the right answer. The next step would be to request a willingness to consciously open this sector of life made visible to the kenotic Christ.

For good reason, this exercise may produce confusion. For starters, disciples are told to trust God at all times. Yet when the Word provokes such dramatic reactions, the question may come: "Do I really trust that Jesus has my best interests in mind when I hear . . . ?" Inner contradictions may materialize: "I *try* to follow, Jesus; I *want* to trust. You've gone too far. . . ." The door slams shut. A startling defensiveness appears unbidden.

Such hostile self-protectiveness tends to surface when we feel threatened, even in the wake of oaths to be more like Christ.

When we hear the Word so clearly intruding upon whichever places we protect, we fear being dragged beyond our comfort zones. We crash headlong against the threat of losing our turf. We secure fortifications against the Word and whoever presumes to threaten our security. We default to self-preservation. The reaction may sound something like this: "I will protect my life! I will create my safe fortress! I will become invulnerable to pain and impenetrable to sorrow." What a tangle arises when the Living Word unearths my resistance to Love Outpoured and I realize I have, shall we say, serious trust issues with God! "I'm resisting the Word of God—now what? Am I going to hell?"

We can feel bewildered or disturbed when we notice how sharply we react to protect our lives, to preserve the status quo, and to ward off calls to change. It can be even more perplexing with the discovery of how intensely we require God to safeguard everything we own and to guarantee we won't have to pluck out eyes or lop off hands. It can indeed be immensely disconcerting when the Word speaks and we recognize how we stand fortified against the exact kind of vulnerability required for anyone to remain truly secure in God. *Quidquid recipitur*. The Word's ability to summon disciples-in-training to a deeper attunement with Outpouring Love intensifies as we grow in our capacity to name our resistances and to recognize more clearly where to welcome the kenotic Christ.

One might respond, "This strikes me as negative. Why do we have to deal with all this negativity?" Why, indeed? It seems to me that our basic choice lies between hypocrisy and integrity. For as long as we deny the resistances that distance us from God, self, and others, we risk remaining trapped in blindness and Pharisaism. I hope that two early objectives of my approach are clearer now. The first, is that as we mature in faith, disciples-in-training grow in the capacity to observe and name emotional responses to Christ. The second is that as we move out of concealment, we see ourselves with greater clarity and welcome Christ as we are. When we are able to name our responses and see ourselves with greater clarity, we can engage with and be engaged by Love Outpoured as we truly are. I believe it will then be possible to integrate even the harshest feelings, attitudes, and experiences into our real presence to the Real Presence.

Let us now explore how another liturgical gesture directs us to be really present for an encounter with the Paschal Mystery by helping us name basic human hungers with greater clarity and discover where we need to welcome Christ's saving presence.

CHAPTER FOUR

Jesus' Temptations in Light of the Hungers of the Human Heart

Oh, late have I loved you; O late have I turned,
Turned from seeking you in creatures,
Fleeing grief and pain within.

O Beauty, Ever Ancient, O Beauty Ever New
You, the mirror of my life renewed:
Let me find my life in you!

"O Beauty Ever Ancient"
O Beauty Ever Ancient (87245) © 2004, Robert F. O'Connor, SJ,
Published by OCP, 5536 NE Hassalo, Portland, OR 97213.
All rights reserved. Used with permission.

My purpose in exploring our very human, yet often overlooked, barriers to the kenotic Christ is to engage Love Outpoured with less pretense. I wish to light a way for encountering the Real Presence that arises from our real presence. We saw earlier how a mindful encounter with the Word and other liturgical gestures or symbols has the capacity to elicit defensive reactions geared to protect our vulnerable selves from conformity to the kenotic Christ.

By maintaining an awareness of such responses, we learn to notice and map out the parts of our previously hidden inner lives.

Before we explore our engagement with the Real Presence of the Body and Blood of Christ, it will be helpful to examine the mystery of human hungers. Our hungers surge forth, not to protect us but to drive us to fill our empty selves. For what do we hunger? What does it mean to be hungry? To be fed? To be fed in the divine banquet? Let us investigate.

Luke's presentation of Jesus' fast in the desert is a good starting point for our exploration of hunger. What reactions surface when we fast? Initially, most of us become preoccupied with food. We want to fill our bellies, pure and simple. I propose that this fixation, our craving for food, relates analogously to the inner, spiritual void revealed when we fast. Our hunger has a voracious demand to be satisfied. Just as in the movie *Little Shop of Horrors*, our spirits shout out, "Feed me!" In the same way that fasting from food leads to hunger and to preoccupation with food, so too our inner hollowness produces a craving that fixates us on almost any sort of remedy.

Human beings hunger for what we perceive to be good for us, whether or not the substance is healthy. For example, when hungry, we can choose to satisfy our appetite either with an apple or a bag of cookies. Many motivations come into play as we choose between healthy food and comfort food.

We can apply this insight to other personal choices by asking questions such as: Why do I want this? What compels me? Really, what truly satisfies? What price do I pay if I fast from pursuing it? Such an approach can help us clarify our spiritual desires (for intimacy, meaning, security, peace, happiness, etc.) and uncover what we really seek. As this chapter unfolds, please notice whether Jesus' fast has anything to reveal about the impact of hunger on our capacity to encounter Love Outpoured.

Jesus and the Hungers of the Human Heart

To delve into the mystery of human hunger, we'll look at Jesus' first temptation:

> And Jesus, full of the Holy Spirit, returned from the Jordan and was led by the Spirit in the desert, forty days being tempted by the devil. He ate nothing in those days, and when they were completed, he hungered. So the devil said to him, "If you are the Son of God, speak to this stone in order that it become a loaf (of bread)." Jesus answered him, "It has been written, that 'A person [*anthrōpos*] lives not on bread only.'"

(Luke 4:1–4; my translation)

Jesus ate nothing for forty days and he hungered. That is obvious, as fasting produces physical hunger. Yet, what if Luke intended that we pay attention to all human hungers? In other words, what if Jesus' hunger manifests the elemental hungers of the human heart? Were that accurate, Luke's narrative could apply more tellingly to worshippers in First World countries today. It would then uncover the temptations we face with food certainly, but with more than food as well. Let us examine the passage closely.

The Lucan narrative indicates that Jesus' temptations follow from the promptings of the Holy Spirit. It seems to be God's will, therefore, that Jesus' desires be tested like gold in the fire before he begins to minister.

We hear that Jesus was hungry. I propose that Jesus' physical hunger operates as a metaphor for the deeper hungers of the human heart. Inasmuch as this is so, we can find consolation in the fullness of his humanity, the mystery of his kenosis, and the depth of his experience of everything human. Thus, if we can associate our experiences of hunger and temptation today with Jesus' hunger and temptation then, we might make his seem less otherworldly and ours more significant.

The key to the passage stands out when we examine its Greek sentence structure. We see then that it says: "Speak to this stone in order that it become a loaf." Looking at this translation, we see that Jesus was not tempted to use his divine power to work magic here. Rather, he was tempted, as we are, to make one thing be what it can never be! In other words, the tempter enticed Jesus to say or treat one thing as if it were something else. This is one shrewd tactic of the enemy of human nature to tempt each of us, in our hunger, to make one good thing be something it can never be. For example, food is a good thing in itself. It is meant to nourish us and provide energy. Many of us, however, are tempted to make food fill our emptiness, ease our pain, or comfort us in our sorrows. It's not made to help us avoid these feelings.

However, Jesus, even while hungry, recognized a stone for what it was—a marvel of creation, a gift that proclaims the graciousness of God in its own way. And at the same time, he understood it was not "fruit of the earth and work of human hands" in the manner of bread. Because of this, the temptation did not work! Why? Since Jesus knew himself as beloved of God, he was neither repelled by his human hunger nor compelled by it. Because he knew he was beloved of God, he did not resent the limitations of created things; he honored them. Jesus, beloved of God, was fully human, having emptied himself of godliness. Jesus' clearsightedness, in spite of his hunger, allowed him to distinguish between one good thing and another good thing. Jesus endured his hunger. He was not conned. Jesus declined to pretend a stone was bread.

How do we react to temptation? Now, most of us would not mistake a stone for bread, no matter how hungry, right? Just about anyone can see the world of difference between them. Who wants to wreck one's teeth pretending they're the same? Yet this most elemental ploy of the tempter is what we fall for as we desperately try to escape hunger. "Treat this stone as if it were bread." Or, in other words, "treat alcohol, sex, drugs, shopping, food, etc., as something you want to fill and nurture you." By the way, it will never do that. Many of us find that when we're hungry, our track record on making this critical differentiation isn't very good. Why?

The Collision of Good Desires and Human Hungers: Learning about Ourselves

When we hunger for God, peace, love, or joy, our deep hunger can lead us to God. Or it can lead us to make use of creatures falsely. Our hunger can blind us to the simple beauty of anything. That is why I understand hunger as equivalent, metaphorically speaking of course, to loneliness, need, emptiness, incompleteness, and vulnerability. Picture these primal forces emanating from an internal Grand Canyon, that profoundly empty crevice that often catches our attention after a profound loss or disillusionment. When our particular cavernous reality appears, each of us is sorely tempted to fill it with anything that will ease the pain.

In so many ways, the real power of hunger comes from the urgency of its demand. Loneliness gnaws at one, driving her to fill this void. Emptiness torments another, compelling him to feed his void. These cravings, these impulses, skew our fundamental perception of reality. They coerce us to frantically require of created things a gratification they can never deliver. Therapeutically speaking, counselors refer to chronic overuse of things as addictions. Theologically, the Church understands these compulsions under the heading of concupiscence, an ancient notion that describes the powerful undertow of sinfulness strong enough to distort our judgment. Scripturally, hunger signifies demand.

We can study the effects of human hunger on our choices by reviewing our experience. If we don't know an addict personally, most of us probably know someone who acts compulsively. The point is that all of us are tempted to require one fundamentally good thing to function as if it were another good thing.

For example, relationships can be wonderful and a source of comfort. Relationships create an environment for receiving and giving, for growing in loving kindness, and for blessing and being blessed. Nonetheless, when we use a relationship to relieve the pain of loneliness, we end by requiring too much of the other, punishing her or him for not satisfying our needs. Relationships, rather, have inherent limitations. They cease to nourish when we coerce another to fill our abyss.

Work is good. It can be energizing. It calls forth creativity and offers an avenue for meaningful self-expression for the good of others. Yet overworking can never fill that vacant place in our gut. It's not meant for that. As surely as a stone is not bread, over-work does not remove hollowness.

Alcohol is good in itself. Relief from pain is another good. A bit of wine heightens conversation. Beer and brats with friends brighten a summer evening. But when we use alcohol (or drugs, etc.) to eliminate the existential angst of life, we fail to achieve the desired end. Instead, we wreak havoc in the process. Compulsively drinking to excess can never take away physical, mental, or spiritual pain. It's just not designed to do that. There's a stone; there's bread.

The same can be said of food. Food is good, sometimes very good! Taking in calories provides energy for the human body. A special dinner nurtures love and friendship. Yet, overeating cannot make up for the unfulfilled or empty spaces in our lives. The short-lived comfort compulsive overeating brings eventually leads to multiple health maladies and neuralgic issues with self-esteem.

Shopping is good. People who keep a home and family need things. Still, excessive shopping can never fill the incompleteness of life.

The list goes on and on. I leave it to the reader to apply this framework to sexuality, surfing the Internet, religion, security, independence, watching television, etc.

I think you catch my drift. Any good thing in this world can be co-opted by the hungers of the human heart and twisted. Even the most altruistic desires can be hijacked and distorted by cravings. When we overuse any created thing habitually, we get hooked. We become dependent in some manner. We develop a pattern of forcing good things to gratify longings they were never designed to satisfy. Work is not meant to take away the sting of loneliness. Food is not intended to replace the comfort of relationships. Alcohol can never help avoid the pain of grief or resentment. Shopping doesn't take away emptiness.

Whether it has to do with religious practices or sex, overworking or alcohol, yielding to the temptation "resolves" some tension, providing temporary relief. But when tension reboots and the pressure from emptiness, loneliness, or privation resurfaces, the all-too-human urge to resolve the tension reappears. That's concupiscence at work. Therefore, the telling question disciples-in-training need to ask is: What price would we pay if we didn't use creatures improperly when driven by hunger's impulse? In reality, we would each shoulder our loneliness, emptiness, or privation, bearing the truth of our reality. That's what Jesus did. He willingly bore the load.

The Collision of Good Desires and Deep Hungers: Learning about Jesus

As Hebrews 4:15 notes, Jesus was "tested as we are" but did not sin. Jesus was tempted to make a stone satisfy his hunger. However, Jesus could differentiate. He respected the limitations and the incompleteness of that unpretentious bit of God's creation. Someone might use stone for building a wall or a walkway in a garden. Another could skip it across a lake. Yet another may use a large, sculpted stone to decorate the yard. But if anyone tries to eat it, look out! A stone never nourishes. It's not bread; it's a stone, for goodness' sake! Again, Jesus could distinguish between what a stone could and could not do because he trusted God even when starving.

Jesus made a choice when he endured the temptation to treat a stone as bread. What consequences flowed from his clarity of sight? *Jesus elected to dwell fully in the incompleteness that abides in the heart of the world.* He opted to pitch his tent in the poverty of human life. He chose to accept the unfinished and imperfect nature of all that is. And by doing that, he embraced his humanity, accepting its grief and disappointment as much as its delight and joy. Or better, he set out on the oceans of life and braved its harshest storms. Jesus rejected living on the surface and thus, he embraced joy and sorrow as one. Clearsighted, knowing well his chasm, he welcomed sorrow with equanimity because he did not despise creation for its limitations.

Finally, the point of Luke's passage isn't "moderation in all things," nor is it "conquer all temptations." Either interpretation reduces the Gospel to sound bites. Rather, Luke invites us, tempted as we are to confuse one thing for another, to account for the ways our most God-ward intentions can be bent by deep processes. When loneliness distorts our good purposes, we are called to dwell within it and endure its effects. When fear of the void co-opts our relationships with things, Christ invites us to remain with our fears courageously. When need warps our willingness to notice the poor, we are called to grieve with Christ the mystery of our poverty. This practice is challenging.

We turn now to examine thirst as a distinct metaphor for the inner urges influencing our choices. Our study of the Woman at the Well (John 4) will instruct us on how to discern what truly satisfies.

CHAPTER FIVE

The Woman at the Well and Human Thirst

My unloveliness I ran from, turned to seek you in all things,
Things you fashioned as a pathway,
Yet I lost myself in them

This created world is glorious, yet I could not see within;
See your loveliness behind all, find the Giver in the Gift.

O Beauty, Ever Ancient, O Beauty Ever New
You, the mirror of my life renewed:
Let me find my life in you!

"O Beauty Ever Ancient"
O Beauty Ever Ancient (87245) © 2004, Robert F. O'Connor, SJ,
Published by OCP, 5536 NE Hassalo, Portland, OR 97213.
All rights reserved. Used with permission.

B iblical writers used *thirst* to represent the deep human longing for that which is good, wise, and divine. The psalmist compares the deer's thirst for water to his own longing for God (Psalm 42). Isaiah summoned the thirsty to "come to the waters. / . . . / Why do you spend your money for that which is not bread,/ and your labor for that which does not satisfy?" (55:1–2). Jesus said that those who thirst for righteousness were blessed (see Matthew 5:6). The fact that thirst can be so compelling—a person needs water for physical life—relates to our inner yearning for goodness, wisdom, and God. Yet, naturally arising is the question: why does the human yearning for such exalted realities seem to fall so short so often?

We might wonder what disciples-in-training can learn from what we know of thirst. Before we explore the story of the Samaritan woman in John's Gospel account, let us turn to a brief investigation of physical dehydration to better comprehend thirst as a metaphor.

The Physiological Effects of Thirst: Fathoming a Metaphor

When we thirst, we experience a dryness in our mouth and a craving for fluid. Lack of fluids and an increase in the concentration of salt in the body stimulates the thirst response: drink water now! Thirst may result from various causes: physical exertion, diabetes, diarrhea, blood loss, shock, stimulants (caffeine, amphetamines, etc.), excessive alcohol consumption, vomiting, infectious diseases, malnutrition, hyperglycemia, and fasting. When bodily fluids decrease, the need for water increases.

A water loss of only 1 percent brings about a minor case of dehydration that results in thirst. Constipation, discomfort, dry mouth, or a headache precedes the negligible mood swings, unexplained fatigue, irritability, confusion, lightheadedness, and sometimes insomnia that accompanies dehydration. A slightly greater water loss (5–6 percent) causes grogginess, nausea, headaches, seizures, and fainting. Renal failure can occur with 8 percent of water loss. With substantial water loss (10–15 percent), muscles convulse, skin shrivels and wrinkles, the tongue swells, vision deteriorates, and mental confusion devolves into disorientation, delirium, and loss of consciousness. If 15 percent or more of a body's fluid is lost, an individual usually dies.

These physiological facts of dehydration teach us several things about the adequacy of thirst as a metaphor for moments in our spiritual lives. First, our demand for water signals a yearning for a balanced system. Thus, thirst for goodness, wisdom, and God indicates our search for holiness through restored equilibrium.

Second, thirst affects not only our bodies but our moods; the greater the lack of water, the greater the emotional impact. Thirsty individuals progress from irritability to fatigue, from confusion to lethargy, and from delirium to death. This continuum of thirst, then, signifies a growing impairment of capacity to make good decisions. Such deficiencies cause greater distance from God, self, and others.

The metaphorical application of these physiological effects generates several questions: What does the quality of participation look like when thirsty disciples enter liturgy? How might thirst shape what we require of worship? What sort of engagement with Christ would slake our spiritual thirst?

Turning to John 4:5–18, we will tease out some significant meaning from the original wording.

Jesus and the Woman of Samaria

So [Jesus] came to a Samaritan city called Sychar, near the plot of
ground that Jacob had given to his son Joseph. Jacob's well (*pēgē*)
was there, and Jesus, tired out by his journey, was sitting by the well
(*pēgē*). It was about noon.

A Samaritan woman came to draw water, and Jesus said to her,
"Give me a drink." (His disciples had gone to the city to buy food.)
The Samaritan woman said to him, "How is it that you, a Jew,
ask a drink of me, a woman of Samaria?" (Jews do not share things
in common with Samaritans.) Jesus answered her, "If you knew
the gift of God, and who it is that is saying to you, 'Give me a drink,'
you would have asked him, and he would have given you living
water." The woman said to him, "Sir, you have no bucket, and the
well (*phrear*) is deep. Where do you get that living water? Are you
greater than our ancestor Jacob, who gave us the well (*phrear*),
and with his sons and his flocks drank from it?" Jesus said to her,
"Everyone who drinks of this water will be thirsty (*dipsaō*) again,
but those who drink of the water that I will give them will never
be thirsty. The water that I will give will become in them a spring
(*pēgē*) of water gushing up to eternal life." The woman said to
him, "Sir, give me this water, so that I may never be thirsty (*dipsaō*)
or have to keep coming here to draw water."

Jesus said to her, "Go call your husband and come back." The woman
answered him, "I have no husband." Jesus said to her, "You are right
in saying, 'I have no husband'; for you have had five husbands, and the
one you have now is not your husband. What you have said is true!"

(John 4:5–18)

The writer of the Fourth Gospel used select terms that resonated both within the Gospel itself and passages in the Septuagint (LXX), the first translation of the Old Testament into Greek. John also employed distinct words that would direct hearers to the Gospel and LXX passages to create certain resonances. Let's study three key words highlighted in the passage above.

Well: *pēgē*

Pēgē occurs three times in John's account of the Gospel, and only in chapter 4. When the occurrences of *pēgē* are read together, the word reveals Jesus as the fountain, the spring of water gushing up in the person toward eternal life. Well, spring, fountain, and flowing stream refer to the person of Jesus. This is apparent in John 4:14: "But those who drink of the water that I will give them will never be thirsty. The water that I will give will become in them a spring (*pēgē*) of water gushing up to eternal life."

Consulting an LXX concordance, we catch some intriguing relationships that affect our interpretation. Five streams of meaning contribute to the depth of John 4. First, the Creator not only makes physical springs of water but is revealed as the Source, the fountain of all life. We see this illustrated in the psalms a number of times, for example: "For with you is the *fountain* of life; / in your light we see light" (Psalm 36:9); "You make *springs* gush forth in the valleys; / they flow between the hills" (Psalm 104:10).

Second, in the psalms, thirst is correlated directly with the yearning of the soul to gaze upon the face of God as we see in Psalm 42:1: "As a deer longs for *flowing (pēgē)* streams, / so my soul longs for you, O God. / My soul thirsts for God, for the living God." John alerts us to the Samaritan woman's as-yet-unidentified longing for God. Her thirst led her to encounter Jesus, who eventually slaked her thirst with the true water of life. Having drunk from the living water, she proclaimed the deeds of God to her people by recounting what Jesus had done for her.

Third, the divine transformation of the earth (rock, flint, burning sand, thirsty ground, dry land, etc.) serves as a metaphor for the graceful transformation of the hardened heart. We could infer that the Samaritan woman was not only thirsty (five husbands), but that her heart had hardened as well, a telling sign of intense spiritual dehydration. An example of God transforming the dry earth is found in Isaiah 41:18: "I will open rivers on the bare heights, / and *fountains* in the midst of the valleys; / I will make the wilderness a pool of water, / and dry land springs of water." (See other such references in Psalm 114:7–8 and Isaiah 35:7.)

Fourth, Isaiah promises, as we see in 58:11, that the springs of water will guide, satisfy, and strengthen Israel on its journey back from exile: "The LORD will guide you continually, / and satisfy your needs in parched places, / and make your bones strong; / and you shall be like a watered garden, / like a spring (*pēgē*) of waters, whose waters never fail." (See also 49:10.) In like manner, Jesus, the well, will guide, satisfy, and strengthen the Samaritan woman and any who accompany her to draw water from this source.

Finally, the prophetic use of *pēgē* reveals Israel's predicament of whether to go to the fountain of living water or seek out the empty cisterns. In Jeremiah 2:13, we read that the people have committed two evils: "they have forsaken me, / the *fountain* of living water, / and dug out cisterns for themselves, / cracked cisterns / that can hold no water." (Similar references to forsaking the fountain provided are in Jeremiah 17:13 and Baruch 3:12.) Jesus called for this most basic discernment from the Samaritan woman, just as he does from disciples-in-training today. Like her, we often wonder where we actually will go to draw water.

Cistern/pit: *phrear*

Phrear occurs twice in John 4. Three streams of meaning flow from the LXX that deepen our interpretation of this passage. First, God relegates the bloodthirsty and the treacherous to the pit (cistern). The Samaritan woman returned constantly to the *phrear,* thus demonstrating her status as a sinner. The psalmist uses this image in Psalm 55:23: "But you, O God, will cast them down / into the lowest pit (cistern); / the bloodthirsty and treacherous / shall not live out half their days." Second, in Psalm 69:14–15, the psalmist relates finding himself in the pit, sinking in the mire, threatened by the flood, surrounded by the deep: "Rescue me from sinking in the mire; / let me be delivered from my enemies / and from the deep waters. / Do not let the flood sweep over me, / or the deep swallow me up, / or the Pit (cistern) close its mouth over me." Does such a description indicate depression? It is certainly possible to speculate on the desolation of the Samaritan woman. It's also conceivable that she is perennially stuck and overwhelmed by emptiness in the midst of "plenty" (five husbands). Third, the theme of discernment appears again, this time emphasizing the shame, dismay, and continued dissatisfaction of those who seek water only at the *phrear*. Even though the cistern is empty, the Samaritan woman repeatedly sought fulfillment (five husbands). Jesus revealed to her the folly of returning to the *phrear*. His words are salvific and she rejoiced to discover her foolishness in the presence of the *pēgē*. The prophet Jeremiah writes, too, of those who had nothing to show for having gone to the cistern, stating, "Her nobles send their servants for water; / they come to the *cisterns*, / they find no water, / they return with their vessels empty. / They are ashamed and dismayed / and cover their heads" (14:3). (See also Jeremiah 2:13.)

To thirst: *dipsaō*

The verb *dipsaō* occurs six times in John's account of the Gospel, with three of these occurrences in chapter 4. The Samaritan woman begins to sense a difference between the two sources of water (*pēgē* and *phrear*). In 4:13–15, she requests *satisfying* water so she will never thirst: "Jesus said to her, 'Everyone who drinks of this water will be thirsty again, but those who drink of the water that I will give them will never be thirsty. The water that I will give will become in them a spring of water gushing up to eternal life.' The woman said to him, 'Sir, give me this water, so that I may never be thirsty or have to keep coming here to draw water.'"

Again, we will consider the several resonances with the LXX. First, as we see in Psalms 42 and 63, the psalmist thirsts for God while experiencing the divine absence. His soul faints for lack of water.

My soul thirsts for God,
    for the living God.
When shall I come
    and behold the face of God?
My tears have been my food
    day and night,
while people say to me continually,
    "Where is your God?"

(42:2–3)

O God, you are my God, I seek you,
    my soul thirsts for you;
my flesh faints for you,
    as in a dry and weary land
        where there is no water.

(63:1)

Second, the prophet Isaiah identifies those who resist God as thirsty people, living in illusion, dreaming about water when he states, "Just as when a hungry person dreams of eating / and wakes up still hungry, / or a *thirsty* person dreams of drinking / and wakes up faint, still *thirsty,* / so shall the multitude of all the nations be that fight against Mount Zion" (Isaiah 29:8). In a similar way, the Samaritan woman lived in a fantasy world, dreaming about flowing water. She awoke perpetually thirsty until she encountered the true *pēgē.*

Third, oppressed by moderate dehydration from wandering in desert wastes, some of the people of Israel grew quarrelsome (see Exodus 17:1–17). They cried to the Lord and through divine intervention were hydrated. Similarly, the Samaritan woman came to Jesus in her distress, seeking freedom from the thirst that plagued her. Disciples-in-training discover the fidelity of God today when we encounter Christ in our thirst.

Fourth, as we see in Isaiah 41:18, Isaiah prophesied a divine reconstruction of the desert, when God will change wild and waste into springs of water: "I will open rivers on the bare heights, / and fountains in the midst of the valleys; / I will make the wilderness a pool of water, / and the dry (*dipsaō*) land springs of water." (See also Isaiah 48:21.) When the Samaritan woman met Jesus in her wilderness, she was transformed by the encounter. Jesus met her where she was, not where she had pretended to be.

Finally, a glance at the other three occurrences of *dipsaō* in John yields significant resonances. The word is used in the Bread of Life discourse: "I am the bread of life. Whoever comes to me will never be hungry, and whoever believes in me will never be *thirsty*" (6:35). Belief slakes thirst! In the next instance, the Samaritan woman also proved this saying by answering Jesus' call to drink with faith. She was the first to discover how the *pēgē* becomes a river (*potamos*) rushing out from the belly of the believer. And finally in John 19:28–30, in his thirst, Jesus, now glorified on the Cross, hands over the Spirit (as promised in John 7:39) with descriptions of thirst, *dipsaō*: "After this, when Jesus knew that all was now finished, he said (in order to fulfill the scripture), 'I am thirsty.' A jar full of sour wine was standing there. So they put a sponge full of the wine on a branch of hyssop and held it to his mouth. When Jesus had received the wine, he said, 'It is finished.' Then he bowed his head and handed over his spirit."

Recall how the human body relies on fluids for health, consciousness, and sanity. Dehydration can disorient individuals, mildly to mortally; therefore, thirst proves to be an effective metaphor to help us discriminate between compulsive forays to empty cisterns and the encounter with Living Water Outpoured.

The Samaritan woman shows us the power of thirst. She returned habitually to the cistern (*phrear*), unable to slake her thirst. Her inability to establish fulfilling relationships (five husbands) shows this. She met Jesus (*pēgē*), who invited her to distinguish between her routine for drawing water and the flowing, life-giving waters he offered. She saw. She drank. With a newfound freedom, she proclaimed joyfully to her village: "He told me everything I have ever done!" She had shame no longer; she told of what she had gained from her encounter with Christ. She is indeed the model disciple in John's account of the Gospel.

Our investigation of the LXX contexts for the three key terms from John 4:5–15 reveals how the misguided behaviors we use to slake our thirst mask a longing for God we have yet to fully reckon. We might want to ask ourselves the following: Can we risk trusting the Creator to transform dry desert into *pēgē*? Are we willing to encounter Outpouring Love and abandon worn paths to personal and corporate cisterns? Are we willing to hazard the revelation that our thirst may have already chained us to deceptive cisterns?

Could we accept Jesus' invitation to drink deeply of the waters of life Christ offers today?

The Eucharistic liturgy is the place to take these questions. How do hunger and thirst manifest themselves in a community's presence at liturgy? What impact could thirst have on a congregation's capacity to engage with the Word? How might thirst influence an assembly's ability to choose to live by Christ's vision? To receive the gift of Living Water Outpoured, what price do we pay to surrender distorted notions that support our crazy-making compulsions? In other words, do we dare risk a transformative encounter with the Paschal Mystery?

CHAPTER SIX

Alienation as Exile, Hypocrisy as Hiding

The problem of talking about liturgy as reflecting and celebrating our experience of life is that, too often, we have no real awareness of what that experience is. Too often we are not sufficiently in touch with what is happening in our own lives for the liturgy to be able to speak to that experience. I suspect that alienation from the liturgy, which many people feel is, in good part at least, a reflection of their own alienation from themselves, and consequently an inability to "resonate" with the language and symbols of the liturgical rite.

Mark Searle[8]

Liturgical theologian Mark Searle singled out what I will call "alienation from self" as the key, underlying pressure that negatively influences worshippers' capacity for participating fully and consciously in liturgical prayer. For Searle, alienation from self is manifested as a compromised ability to engage Outpouring Love due to an inability to "resonate" with the language and symbols of the liturgical rite. Consequently, the ritual's power to mediate life-giving relationships among God, self, and others is diminished. Alienation unequivocally reduces our basic availability to be conformed to Christ.

The Russian Orthodox theologian Alexander Schmemann likewise lamented the current disconnect with liturgical prayer:

> The liturgy . . . has ceased to be connected with virtually all other aspects of the Church's life; to inform, shape and guide the ecclesiastical consciousness as well as the "worldview" of the Christian community. One may be deeply attached to [the rituals] . . . and, at the same time fail to see in them the totality of the Church's *leitourgia*, an all-embracing vision of life, a power meant to judge, inform, and transform the whole of existence, a "philosophy of life" shaping and challenging all our ideas, attitudes and actions. . . . Liturgy is neither explained nor understood as having anything to do with "life"; as above all, an *icon* of that new life which is to challenge and renew that "old life" within us and around us.[9]

We know the familiar laments that are raised about contemporary Roman Catholic liturgy. Banal celebrations, symbols rendered mute, loss of transcendence, feeble response to the breadth of the Church's social teaching, wearisome preaching, excessively informal or formal rituals, and passive congregations are but a few of the complaints. But do these problems have to do only with liturgy? I wonder if it's easier to blame the rite while overlooking our personal and corporate alienation. I find Ronald Rolheiser's description of alienation helpful in illuminating what we are dealing with:

> [Alienation] refers simply to the experience of feeling alienated or estranged from others. . . . When relationships are inadequate to the point of being painful and frustrating to us, we suffer alienation.

Many factors cause alienation: for example, fear, shame, lack of self-esteem, paranoia, ideological differences with others, positive rejection by others, physical handicaps, emotional handicaps, physical separation from others, or anything else that hinders us from relating as closely and intimately to others as we would like.[10]

Disconnected from God, self, and others, alienated individuals feel detached. They may experiences separation, estrangement, and distance from family, friends, Church, or society. They habitually withdraw, sensing they don't belong. They shore up fortifications to protect their vulnerable selves and become highly defensive. The catch-22 is that the defensiveness impedes the very intimacy they seek.

What, then, are the odds that worshippers heavily invested in conscious or unconscious self-protection would be able or willing to open to God, self, and others their tender, guarded places? Wouldn't they instead react aggressively to protect their turf? We would be right to assume that anyone caught in such a cycle of self-protective maneuvers would find relating vulnerably to others quite challenging.

Biblically Speaking, Alienation Is Exile

> My soul is downcast within me;
> therefore I remember you
> from the land of the Jordan and of Hermon,
> from Mount Mizar,
> Deep calls to deep
> at the thunder of your cataracts;

all your waves and your billows
>> have gone over me.
By day the Lord commands his steadfast love,
>> and at night his song is with me,
>> a prayer to the God of my life.
I say to the God, my rock,
>> "Why have you forgotten about me?
Why must I walk about mournfully
>> because the enemy oppresses me?"
As with a deadly wound in my body,
>> my adversaries taunt me,
while they say to me continually,
>> "Where is your God?"
Why are you cast down, O my soul,
>> and why are you disquieted within me?
Hope in God; for I shall again praise him,
>> my help and my God.

(Psalm 42:6–11)

Whether refugee or immigrant, high school goth or college nerd, skateboarder or soccer mom, survivalist or farmer, anorexic or jock, one whose sexual orientation puts her on the margins of society or a dad going through a midlife crisis, persons on the edge of what is deemed "normal" suffer disengagement from life, detachment from self, or distance from others. Life on the periphery entails alienation. What ought be said, then, to a disciple-in-training who, in the depths of alienation, asks, *why*?

Too often, the responses to this pained question are trite: "God must have wanted this," "you deserved . . . ," or "someday it will all make sense." The experience of alienation merits more than clichés.

I translate "why" not as a request for an answer but as a statement registering anguish. People of faith can honor this anguish by linking this gut-driven *why* to biblical stories. A particularly powerful one is that of Judah's exile from Jerusalem followed by the destruction of the city and Temple (sixth century BC). The story reveals something basic about alienation. This period of devastating loss saw divine promises and symbols of the covenant shattered. Hostages taken to Babylon languished for years, stigmatized by divine abandonment. These refugees were utterly forsaken, disillusioned by the annihilation of nation and temple, hearth and home. Then, a prophet spoke to them. God sent the individual that scholars refer to as Second Isaiah (Isaiah 40—55) to call those exiles home. Isaiah still speaks today to anyone overwhelmed by loss, abandonment, or betrayal and facing life on the margins. Consider the type of reply the prophet's words call forth in the following passage:

> When the poor and the needy seek water,
>> and there is none,
>> and their tongue is parched with thirst,
> I the LORD will answer them,
>> I the God of Israel will not forsake them,
> I will open rivers on the bare heights,
>> and fountains in the midst of the valleys;
>> I will make the wilderness a pool of water,
>> and the dry lands springs of water.

(41:17–18)

Why does God go to the trouble of sponsoring a massive landscaping project in the desert? Why raise the valleys? Why lower the mountains? Why make springs flow through the desert for the thirsty?

Recall that Second Isaiah addressed refugees in Babylon. The Word *then* was aimed at making the way inviting and safe for the exiles to return: "When you pass through the waters, I will be with you" (43:2). Second Isaiah summoned Israel, calling the people back from Babylon *then*. This same Word addresses disciples-in-training in our experience of alienation *today,* beckoning us to return to God. The Word bids us to trust.

We will attend to Isaiah's summons by considering several familiar passages and truthfully record our responses to them. In the texts from Isaiah that we read during Advent, I propose that the prophet addressed the Word to exiles then, and to the alienated today. How do you respond to the Word?

> [The Lord] gives power to the faint,
> and strengthens the powerless.
> Even youths will faint and be weary,
>   and the young will fall exhausted;
> but those who wait for the Lord shall renew their strength,
>   they shall mount up with wings like eagles,
> they shall run and not be weary,
>   they shall walk and not faint.

(40:29–31)

But now, thus says the LORD,
he who created you, O Jacob,
    he who formed you, O Israel:
Do not fear, for I have redeemed you;
    I have called you by name, you are mine.
Because you are precious in my sight,
    and honored, and I love you,
I give people in return for you,
    nations in exchange for your life.
Do not fear, for I am with you;
    I will bring your offspring from the east,
    and from the west I will gather you.
I will say to the north, "Give them up,"
    and to the south, "Do not withhold;
bring my sons from far away
    and my daughters from the end of the earth.

(43:1, 4–6)

For the LORD has called you
    like a wife forsaken and grieved in spirit,
like the wife of a man's youth when she is cast off,
    says your God.
For a brief moment I abandoned you,
    but with great compassion I will gather you.
In overflowing wrath for a moment
    I hid my face from you;
but with everlasting love I will have compassion on you,
    says the LORD, your Redeemer.
For the mountains may depart
    and the hills be removed,
but my steadfast love shall not depart from you,
    and my covenant of peace shall not be removed,
says the LORD, who has compassion on you.

(54:6–8, 10)

The Word proclaimed *today* can elicit passionate responses from exiles. Please recall your reactions. What did you say when you heard, "Do not fear, for I have redeemed you"; "Do not fear, for I am with you"; "with everlasting love I will have compassion on you"; or, "For a brief moment I abandoned you"? Some might say, "Thanks!" Others could easily say, "Oh, yeah, where were you when . . . ?" "So, when did you change your mind?" or, "You're the one who sent us here. What the . . . !" Just as suffering usually generates mistrust, so, too, alienation spawns suspicion and seething resentment. Did the prophet's words dredge up any wounds of abandonment? Did Isaiah's words uncover personal experiences of betrayal?

It seems to me that many of us who have suffered disillusionment, abandonment, or betrayal find it incomprehensible to respond positively to God or a Church that says, "Never mind what has happened to you in the past because it's all better now! See, I am doing these great deeds for you! Come back! All is well! Return to me!" What changes in our spiritual lives when this Word elicits hurt, resentment, desertion, temptation, or isolation? I believe that trust emerges as *the* spiritual/religious issue for exiles. That is, inasmuch as alienation and exile are related scripturally, trust functions as the fundamental problem for good-yet-wounded, spiritual and religious people.

When mistrust erupts, what are we to do? As a companion in exile, let me tenderly offer this word to those who have undergone profound disappointment or loss and find themselves wandering on the periphery: if and when we wish to return home, whatever that means to us, assistance is available. I believe internal healing can be found in the Liturgical Contemplative Practice that will be outlined in this book, as well as in Twelve-Step spirituality, supportive counseling, spiritual companionship, and other ways.

After a major loss, our relationship with God shifts. Faith once assured us that our questions do not echo meaninglessly. In loss, a different level of questioning surfaces. We may ask: What did I do to deserve this? Will I trust God again after betrayal or disillusionment? Will God accept me even if I mistrust Christ? Will I accept me if I question in anger? Why me? Ouch! I really hate this. Why can't things be the way they used to be? I'm angry.

Many of us were taught as young children that we would be rewarded if we behaved ourselves and were "good." However, believing that children who do as they are told will be protected from misery can lead to resentful isolation, especially from God. Thus alienated, an individual may sever his or her relationship with God completely. Yet, speaking the truth honestly to God and being willing somehow to listen to the Word may result in some sort of letting down of the drawbridge. I hesitate to suggest too much, but I wonder whether hostility needs to be the final word.

Liturgical participation becomes riskier when we recognize that worship itself has the potential to lead us into the depths of our emotions. When we recognize how liturgy has the power to summon us to the brink of life and death, thus anticipating regeneration, we can see that liturgical participation heralds grace.

I realize I propose an ideal that disciples-in-training remain in relationship with God *while isolated, alienated, or still in exile.* I recognize the hazard of having to reenter the pain to regain relationship. The paradox stands that facing and integrating painful parts of our lives into our relationship with God leads to the healing of alienation.

Can Alienation Herald a Return?

Inasmuch as alienation is widespread among individuals and communities, I believe it will do little good to ask what strategies might be employed to overcome alienation from God, self, and others. Instead, I recommend these queries: How can liturgy achieve its purposes when worshippers are not sufficiently in touch with emotionally toned areas of their lives and are oblivious to their inner depths? How can worshippers engage the Paschal Mystery while still resisting awareness of personal alienation and remaining unconscious of secret defensiveness? Or, what are the conditions that liturgy might, in fact, encourage disciples-in-training to encounter Christ meaningfully?

Our relationship with ourselves, others, and God, needs to be from where we are, not from where we wish to be. Our liturgical celebrations do not help us face the emotionally charged truth of our existence (for example, estrangement from God, self, and others) when we shield ourselves from the parts of our lives we wish to avoid. In shielding ourselves, we sidestep our vulnerability and reinforce our alienated stance unawares.

Current approaches to liturgical catechesis offer little remedy. These have proved inadequate for cultivating fruitful, personal engagement with the Paschal Mystery, because they bypass the embodied, emotional lives of real people. Liturgical catechesis often focuses exclusively on what liturgy is in itself, what worshippers ought to do, and the effects liturgy should have on our lives. Liturgy is treated metaphysically. Let me explain.

A metaphysical approach concentrates on a conceptual meaning of liturgy and the results that should follow. It deals with liturgy in terms of universal theory, general principle, and fixed norms. It presumes that following what the Church understands or requires produces meaningful practice. It asks, "What is liturgy in itself?" "What should it do?"

Don't get me wrong. Understanding the rich ideals within liturgical documents is important in preparing and participating in the liturgy. Yet this approach is insufficient. How can disciples-in-training get there (realizing liturgical ideals) from here (our state of alienation)? It's a conundrum. Knowledge of the liturgy does not automatically direct worshippers to a deeper encounter with the Paschal Mystery. However, let's not throw the baby out with the bathwater. We need a method that integrates the emotional responses of Christian worshippers *with* this metaphysical approach. I believe we need both greater emotional awareness and a deeper understanding of our encounter with Christ through liturgical prayer.

Therefore, I invite seekers, activists, the patently religious, the spiritual, the disillusioned, and the jaded, as well as academics, professional liturgists, priest celebrants, deacons, liturgical ministers, persons in the pew, and members of the hierarchy, to weigh the impact of alienation on contemporary liturgical practice and participation. And I propose Liturgical Contemplative Practice as one remedy.

Liturgical Contemplative Practice is a Eucharistic spirituality that situates the Body of Christ squarely within our alienated lives to discover a pathway to engagement with Christ. It promotes an encounter with Christ that cultivates integration of mind and heart, understanding and feeling, and theology and experience.

As we develop an ever-growing, conscious attention to our immediate, emotional responses to Love Outpoured, we will discover we are more genuinely present to God, self, and others. Such real presence of worshippers is an apt response to the Real Presence of Christ. It may seem counterintuitive, but the more we become conscious of the ways we avoid vulnerability, the more we learn mindful, personal presence to the transforming embrace of Christ in liturgical prayer with fewer pretenses and less hypocrisy.

Hypocrisy as Hiding

Woe to you, scribes and Pharisees, hypocrites! For you clean the outside of the cup and the plate, but inside they are full of greed and self-indulgence. You blind Pharisee! First clean the inside of the cup, so that the outside also may become clean. Woe to you, scribes and Pharisees, hypocrites! For you are like our whitewashed tombs, which on the outside look beautiful, but inside they are full of bones of the dead and of all kinds of filth. So you also on the outside look righteous to others, but inside you are full of hypocrisy.

(Matthew 23:25–28)

A hypocrite can be described as an individual who plays a part or pretends. Greek actors were, in actuality, hypocrites. Each played his part on stage wearing a mask. After performing, though, each took off his mask and went to the pub (or wherever ancient Greeks unwound). These early artists seemed to recognize the difference between their stage masks and their real faces.

Jesus was concerned with mask-wearers. The evangelists describe the Pharisees as full-time mask-wearers. Historically speaking, the Pharisees were good lay reformers who sought to make Judaism more relevant to daily living. Some scholars speculate that Jesus may have been a member of the Pharisaic movement. Yet, while sympathetic to their goals, he regularly confronted them, as demonstrated in the parable of the Pharisee and the Publican (Luke 18:9–14). Jesus took the Pharisee to task for portraying himself religiously while remaining willfully and invincibly ignorant of his inner reality. In this parable, we Pharisees probably expect that the hero of the story would be someone just like us. Of course, our expectations are forever upended! Jesus repeatedly challenged them as he still challenges us to stop confusing religious masks with real faces. Jesus constantly challenges hypocrites.

I propose that hypocrisy is always and everywhere the fundamental temptation of good, religious people, whether we wish to call it Pharisaism, pretense, sham, charade, forgery, counterfeit, façade, denial, simulation, make-believe, or deceit. Decent people are tempted every day to pretend they are one way while acting otherwise. Those who avoid standing for anything usually don't have to deal with this tension. Yet, whoever deliberately makes a commitment to God is assured of persistent temptations to simulate virtue and disguise sinfulness and weakness.

In the end we have only one choice, don't we? We can either allow our true selves to be seen or choose hypocrisy. When we choose hypocrisy, we opt for the fabrication of a self that doesn't exist and in so doing, we choose blindness: "I don't want to see myself or be seen!" The living Word, though, calls us from the shadows of night into the Divine Light *now* as Jesus did *then* with the Pharisees! When we allow ourselves to be seen, we make an explicit choice to embrace the singular suffering essential to discipleship.

Alienation from God, self, and others typically leads to isolation and avoidance. You and I have a choice. We can bring our whole selves to liturgy by plunging into the deep waters of vulnerability, or we can opt for hypocrisy.

CHAPTER SEVEN

Liturgy and Our Resistance

Esse est percipi.[11]

Bishop George Berkeley

Being real and present means bringing our whole selves to the encounter with the Paschal Mystery. Let's turn, then, to descriptions of what bringing one's whole self to liturgy looks like.

The eighteenth-century British philosopher Bishop George Berkeley bequeathed to us the tidy saying, *esse est percipi*, "to be is to be perceived." The saying may not explain existence convincingly to a twenty-first century audience, yet it offers a valuable spiritual insight: individuals or communities are "real" insofar as they are willing and able to be seen honestly and completely by another. Its contrapositive, I think, is equally true: to be unseen, to remain hidden, means to be unreal. To the extent that anyone hides from self or conceals portions of his life from God and others, he remains unreal. He skulks in the shadows. He pretends.

We become "real" with Christ when we let him truly see us—when we are truly vulnerable before him and before others. This requires transparency, mutuality, and reciprocity. Liturgy can be a powerful vehicle for drawing us toward greater authenticity with God, self, and others.

Being real in liturgy involves first recognizing who I am, or who we are as a community, with ever greater clarity. This entails being mindful of both gifts and failings. Further, it means naming and admitting those same gifts and faults honestly before God and others. Being real also refers to developing the capacity to bring those same gifts and resistances into each liturgical encounter with the Paschal Mystery. Our presence to God, self, and others is a powerful antidote to the alienation that besets us as we walk a surer pathway toward incarnating liturgy's compelling ideals.

Being real, however, is easier said than done. Whether numbed by monotony or protected by multiple layers of defense, many of us would be hard-pressed to give an honest appraisal of where we are in relationship to the process I've just described. To be truly present, truly real, requires accounting for our present emotional status. What else could *being present* mean other than closely noticing our own movements, including attraction and masquerading in the presence of the kenotic Christ? Without such competence, we live out a vaguely elusive, yet always pervasive charade, otherwise known in religious circles as hypocrisy.

Getting real with God counterbalances alienation, superficiality, and avoidance. Bringing our whole selves to liturgy assists disciples-in-training with this counterbalance. But before discussing how we bring ourselves to the liturgy, let us consider how we hold ourselves back. We will look at three common ways we habitually remain unreal.

Three major temptations sidetrack us from plunging into the depths of our human vulnerability. First, living in denial about the truth of our sinfulness keeps us in the shallows of grace. Second, evaluating the faults of others without including ourselves under the same verdict leaves us in the shadows of judgment. Third, becoming overly absorbed with our sinfulness renders us well fortified against the mercy of God. Each tactic reinforces alienation. When we take up any of these strategies, we end up trying to conceal huge parts of our lives from God (as if that were possible). The strategy for concealment backfires as our sense of estrangement from God, self, and others intensifies.

Denial

Welcoming Love Outpoured may appear to conflict with admitting sinfulness. Shame easily leads us to identify sinfulness with disappointing God, and so we are tempted to avoid being seen.[12] This inclination makes it inordinately attractive to cloak our culpability for anything. Still, our tendency to sin constantly reasserts itself. We bump into our sinful selves over and over again as they bump into others. We are not strong enough to counter the power of concupiscence. We succumb regularly. Many of us, however, find it too painful to acknowledge our status as sinners. Denial helps us bury these experiences.

We practice denial as we compare ourselves favorably to others: "That isn't me." "At least I'm not as bad as . . ." We fend off shame by waving the banner of "at least I'm trying," or we minimize all sins as irrelevant blemishes: "[XYZ] isn't that big a deal. No one's perfect, after all!" We also delve into denial as we bargain with God: "I promise with all my might to be more religious if you . . ." Deny, deny, deny.

No matter the version of denial, the same end is achieved. In practicing denial, we distance ourselves from our experience and relinquish responsibility for our actions. The gap that we create, the very picture of alienation, supports our schemes to remain invisible before Christ. We persist with denial because somehow we have convinced ourselves that relating to God openly as sinful always implies shame. Our refrain may be, "Please don't look at me too closely, God! Please don't make me look at myself!" It is distressingly poignant that avoiding this area of vulnerability frustrates the human longing for relationship and keeps us alienated.

How can we conquer denial? We don't find ourselves where we want to be with God because we habitually present ourselves where we pretend to be. That is, the more we segregate where we want to be from where we are, the more we hide from divine interaction. Ultimately, we play hide and seek with God by nervously taking cover in that place known as *Where We Want Others to See Us*. (It intersects with *I'm Trying*.) We conquer denial, however, by learning to welcome Christ exactly where we are. Our other option is to remain frozen in the shallows, petrified of our vulnerability.

Evaluating Others

We avoid being real by remaining blind to ourselves and our deeper motives. Instead of regarding ourselves as we are, we focus on others' faults while discounting ours. This ploy is reminiscent of the old saying that you're seeing the mote in the eye of another rather than the plank in your own. We practice hypocrisy as we fail to account in our lives for the defects we see in others. It is excruciatingly painful to recognize how blindness to personal failings shapes our estimation of others. And yet, the Word tells us that another person's faults reflect what we avoid in ourselves.

To see more clearly, it will help to differentiate between evaluation and acknowledgment. Evaluation of others leaves us off the hook. When we evaluate others, we point the finger, conveniently excluding ourselves from analysis and critique. We might say or think to ourselves, "Those people are bad, sinful, screwed up, or stupid!" In effect, we are saying, "You are tainted. I see you clearly. I name your defects from the security of my bunker. I judge you and condemn you." Whether our evaluation is somewhat accurate is moot; it represents hypocrisy at its finest.

We hypocrites project a standard on others, focusing on their failures to live up to the standard while neglecting to evaluate ourselves. Often enough, we hypocrites complete our judgment by seeking to hide portions of our lives from God—sometimes behind a mask of religiosity. We obscure *where we are* while exposing only *where we pretend to be*. We can breathe easily because we've seemingly eluded judgment. What is the result? The very human (and sinful) tendency to choose pretense over honest self-disclosure allows us to hide out in *Where We Project We Are* and lurk safely in the shadows.

On the other hand, with "acknowledgment," we intentionally incorporate ourselves into any assessment of others. That is, we profess solidarity with those we evaluate. We judge relationally. Acknowledgment disposes the evaluator toward confession because of the accompanying inclination to admit participation in the faults found in others. This way of perceiving the world keeps the door open to repentance, conversion, and reconciliation because whatever we notice in *them* quickly exposes failings in *us*. We can bring these failings honestly before Love Outpoured and thus step out of the gloomy fog into the Light.

Self-Engrossed

This third temptation is, in some ways, the most insidious yet effective tactic for hiding. This is also referred to as "scrupulosity." Here, individuals become so entangled in personal sins or even the thought of sinning that, in despair, the mercy of God is deflected, rendering grace fruitless for the moment. For the scrupulous, a world of personal fears collapses inward, suffocating them. It is not that they do not have faith; rather, they have become so enthralled, so mesmerized by their failure to break free from the prison of sinfulness on their own that, in effect, they hold salvation at bay. "God will never love me as I am. I am doomed."

Absorbed by the hypnotic intensity of human vulnerability, they remain fretfully fortified against God's saving mercy.

Each of these maneuvers produces similar results. Leaping over sinfulness, vulnerability, judgment, or enmeshment shelters us from a deeper engagement with God in Christ. The pain of being loved explicitly as sinners leads us to pose as "good little boys and girls who do as they are told." Yet, each maneuver shields us from a fully human and liberating encounter with the kenotic Christ, ourselves, or anyone else.

I firmly believe that bringing our whole selves to liturgy serves as the spadework that prepares the ground (attuning ourselves to our emotionally textured experiences) for receiving the seeds of understanding (theological and scriptural study) that will counter what I've just described. Bringing our whole selves to liturgy, to see and be seen by Christ, collides with our basic patterns of avoidance. Bringing our whole selves to liturgical engagement is risky. We face the following questions: Am I willing to surrender my status as alienated? Am I willing to clearly see the tactics I use to stay alienated? Am I able to start recognizing, naming, admitting, and dealing with emptiness, pain, incompleteness, weakness, vulnerability, loneliness, anger, fear, and hunger that impel me to defend myself against a profound encounter with the kenotic Christ? I recognize my fear and resistance as I ask these questions; therefore, I do not inquire into these matters lightly.

CHAPTER 8

A Paradigm for Discipleship

. . . but I grew,
like a pig in a trenchcoat I grew . . .
but I grew, I grew,
and God was there like an island I had not rowed to,
still ignorant of Him, my arms and my legs worked,
and I grew, I grew,
I wore rubies and bought tomatoes
and now, in my middle age,
about nineteen in the head I'd say,
I am rowing, I am rowing
though the oarlocks stick and are rusty
and the sea blinks and rolls
like a worried eyeball,
but I am rowing, I am rowing,
though the wind pushes me back
and I know that that island will not be perfect,
it will have the flaws of life,
the absurdities of the dinner table,
but there will be a door
and I will open it
and I will get rid of the rat inside of me,
the gnawing pestilential rat.
God will take it with his two hands
and embrace it. . . .
This story ends with me still rowing.

"Rowing," *The Awful Rowing Toward God*
Anne Sexton

A mindful encounter with the Paschal Mystery guides disciples-in-training into places of vulnerability and sinfulness where they might encounter the Physician who can heal them, as Anne Sexton so vividly puts it, of the "gnawing pestilential rat." Our doggedly successful sidestepping of the alienated parts of our lives, however, complicates matters. Even though plunging into our depths is the antidote to alienation, superficiality, and hypocrisy, most of us recoil when summoned.

Sadly, religious or family training has led many to reject sinful status due to vivid feelings of self-hatred and low self-esteem. The judgment and punishment that were constant threats for such individuals encouraged them to live as if perpetually on trial before a hypercritical judge and unforgiving jury. Toxic environments as these eventually co-opt the act of admitting sinfulness, commandeering it for other purposes. Shame at failures and imperfections locks a person into a vicious cycle of

acting out → shame/remorse → despair/dejection → isolation → confession → relief → recurrence of tension → repetition of cycle.

Low self-esteem, self-hatred, and preemptive punishment inhabit the middle portion of this process, seducing the sinner into believing that God rejects him because he is not good enough. The fear of being seen as a sinner, much less self-identified as a sinner, then, produces a rigid, monochromatic view of the Christian life blinding individuals to the truth that a disciple's life is a many-sided, ongoing reality.

Spiritual writers throughout the ages witnessed this reality by employing metaphors to illustrate the breadth of the inner life. It is described as a mansion with countless rooms, a voyage across the desert, an ascent to the mountain, an escape through the Red Sea, a passage through hell and purgatory to heaven, a descent into night, and a pilgrimage to a shrine. Such variety suggests that the spiritual life is extraordinarily dynamic. None of these wise, spiritual practitioners reduce it simplistically to polar opposites.

Permit me to offer an additional image. Disciples-in-training approach their interior world as cartographers, surveying the mountains, valleys, seashores, forests, and swamps throughout their inner lives. They write maps to authenticate Christ's sovereign claim over their lives. Their discipleship calls them to explore the heights and depths that affect their conscious and unconscious relationship with God, self, and others.

We disciples in the United States are blessed to live in a time and place in which a broad range of tools exist to chart our inner terrains. Liturgical Contemplative Practice is one such tool. It directs disciples-in-training to reconnoiter interior heights and depths to be present to God. To find out more about this practice and to investigate a model for exploring personal depths, turn with me to a study of the call of Simon Peter.

Jesus Sends Simon Peter to the Depths

Now it came to pass, as the crowd pressed upon him and heard the word of God, he was standing by the lake Gennesaret. And he saw two *ships* (*ploion*) standing by the lake. But the fishermen having gone away from them, were washing the nets. And getting into one of the *ships*, which was Simon's, he asked him to put out a little from the land. And sitting, he taught the crowds from the ship. And when he ceased speaking, he said to Simon: Put out into *the deep* (*bathos*) and let down your nets for a draught. And answering, Simon said: "Master, laboring through the whole night, we took nothing, but at your word I will let down the nets." And this doing, they enclosed a great multitude of fishes and their nets were being torn. And they nodded to their partners in the other ship that they should come to help them. And they filled both ships so that they were sinking. And seeing, Simon Peter fell at the knees of Jesus saying, "Depart from me because I am a sinful man (*anēr amartōlos*) Lord." For astonishment seized him and all the ones with him at the draught of the fishes which they took; and likewise both James and John, sons of Zebedee, who were sharers with Simon.

And Jesus said to Simon, "Fear not. From now on you will be catching people alive (*zōgreō*)." And bringing down the ships onto the land, leaving all things, they followed him.

(Luke 5:1–11; my translation)

Before examining certain words in this text, I would like to note my reliance on the Greek text for this translation. For at least two reasons I devote much attention to the Greek, the language from which the text is translated into English. First, each evangelist built a web of relationships around usages of a word that together connected portions of the Gospel account, thus filling out the term's meaning. It is easier to see this in the Greek. Second, most of the terms so employed also resonate with words used in the Septuagint (LXX), the first translation of the Old Testament into Greek, adding overtones to the New Testament usage. *Ploion*, the first word we will study, usually is translated in English to "boat." Yet that translation misses the various nuances found in *ploion*, "ship," that we find in the LXX.

Points to Notice

Boat/ship: Jesus got into Simon's *ship*, obviously. That is what poor fishermen piloted, right? Recall how after the Resurrection, Jesus (see Luke 24:31) opened the minds of his disciples to understand Moses, the prophets, and the psalms. The author commits his gentile audience to know their Jewish heritage. As we account for the LXX usage of *ploion*, "ship," we find powerful resonances that nuance our common-sense understanding:

> For the LORD of hosts has a day
>> against all that is proud and lofty,
>> against all that is lifted up and high;
> against all the *ships* of Tar'shish,
>> and against all the beautiful craft.
> The haughtiness of people shall be humbled,
>> and the pride of everyone shall be brought low.

> (Isaiah 2:12, 16–17a; see also Ezekiel 27:3–9, 25, 34
> as well as Isaiah 23:1, 14)

The LXX usage adds what I hear as a likely nuance that brings the richness of pride and independence to our view of Simon. This ship ferries Simon to the deep. It takes him to encounter his unrecognized pride and sinfulness that dwell beneath the surface.

The deep: Jesus directed Simon toward a great fishing site, correct? That's the common-sense interpretation. However, notice the following occurrences of the Greek *bathos*, "depths," in the psalms as they appear in the Septuagint. The use of *bathos* directs our attention toward some important scriptural links descriptive of the place Jesus sent Simon:

> Save me, O God,
>   for the waters have come up to my neck.
> I sink in *deep mire* (*bathos*),
>   where there is no foothold;
> I have come into *deep waters* (*bathos*),
>   and the flood sweeps over me.
>
> O God, you know my folly;
>   the wrongs I have done are not hidden from you.
>
> (69:1–2, 5)

> Out of the *depths* (*bathos*) I cry to you, O LORD.
>   Lord, hear my voice!
> Let your ears be attentive
>   to the voice of my supplications!
>
> If you, O LORD, should mark iniquities,
>   Lord, who could stand?
> But there is forgiveness with you,
>   so that you may be revered.
>
> (130:1–4)

These LXX passages inform our interpretation of *the deep*. Jesus didn't just send Simon to the choicest part of the lake to fish. He sent him on a biblical and spiritual plunge into deep waters to discover his sinfulness. Jesus sent Simon somewhere he didn't necessarily want to go.

Sinful man: When Simon Peter saw, he fell at Jesus' knees and exclaimed, "Depart from me, Lord, I am a sinful man." This is not your typical behavior for a seasoned fisherman hauling in a huge catch. It alerts us to look closely at the Greek. An investigation of *anēr amartōlos* ("sinful male") shows its only other appearance in Luke's account of the Gospel (24:7): "It was necessary that the Son of Man be delivered into the hands of sinful *(amartōlos)* men *(anēr)* and be crucified and to rise again on the third day." Here's my reading: Simon Peter had just fathomed the depths of his sinfulness. He *saw*. He cried "Depart from me" because he recognized his iniquities in the deep mire. Simon Peter does not yet realize the full implications of his discovery. Instead, he knows only horror for what he saw in himself in that sacred deep. The author and the audience know, however, that Peter will betray Jesus. This is not about minor faults, small peccadilloes. Simon's profound capacity for treachery comes to light.

Still, there's another curious element. Luke names this disciple Simon *Peter* exactly when he acknowledged his sinfulness in his depths. Isn't it remarkable that, at the very time Simon discovers and confesses he is a sinful man, Luke preemptively names him *Peter*? A ray of sunshine appears. The evangelist portrays Simon's confession of sinfulness as salvific. It is his crucial act of *seeing* (and being seen) that anticipates his eventual healing and transformation.

Save alive: Finally, note what Jesus says to Simon! "From now on you will be *saving people alive*." That's exactly what the Greek says. This translation is somewhat different than "Do not be afraid; from now on you will be catching people" in the New Revised Standard Version (NRSV) and the New American Bible (NAB), which uses "men" instead of "people." Matthew's version (4:19) in the NRSV is, "Follow me, and I will make you fish for people," and in the NAB is, "Come after me and I will make you fishers of men." Luke does not reproduce Matthew. Instead, he uses a highly idiosyncratic verb, *zōgreō*, "to take/catch people alive," an unconventional verb with a fascinating history.

The Book of Joshua (LXX) employs *zōgreō* several times (2:13; 6:25; 9:26). When Israel arrived at Jericho, Joshua sent spies to reconnoiter the city. These spies made contact with a local prostitute (Joshua 2:1). Once Rahab learned that God had put the city under the ban (divine judgment entailing absolute annihilation), she made a deal with them to "save her and her family alive." The Book of Joshua refers at least six times to the way Rahab and her family were *saved alive* (*zōgreō*) from the death sentence.

Jesus replied to Simon's protests, saying, "Fear not." He then tasked Simon with the mission to "save others alive." Simon's journey to the deep and his discovery of his treachery became the source of his mission, of his vocation to "save alive" fellow sinners.

That is, his ministry flowed directly from the saving grace of his encounter in the deep that resulted in his profound recognition of himself as a *sinful man*. From this point forward, he would serve most genuinely when he lived in harmony with this saving engagement! To paraphrase a saying from our Jesuit Constitutions, "The grace that was at work to save Simon is the same grace from which Peter will most authentically serve."[13] This grace comes to fruition very slowly during Simon's walk with Jesus, ultimately only through the gift of the Spirit at Pentecost.

Applying These Insights

When disciples-in-training encounter the Paschal Mystery in liturgy, Christ sends us to our depths to uncover and name whichever powerful undercurrents (concupiscence/hungers/thirsts/sinfulness) drive us. We recognize these currents as old wounds, fears of being seen, or undetected anger. Whatever we discover in our depths is objective data that identifies where we need to welcome Christ. Exposure of sinfulness is not judgment. While it may be greeted with shame, in Liturgical Contemplative Practice, *discovery* means delving into an unprejudiced, dispassionate collection of data from our depths, just as Simon did.

At the same time, not only does this encounter send worshippers to uncover and admit omission and commission, but also to find salvation and receive our vocation. That's what it means to be a sinner! Essentially, three interrelated elements are here: discovering sinfulness, meeting saving grace, and receiving a mission.

If we achieve only remorse or sorrow, then conformity to Christ remains stunted. Only by knowing in our bones that Jesus saves us and sends us on mission do we function most authentically as disciples. It's not about us; it's about seeing ourselves and being seen more clearly by Christ. The psalms proclaim God is our safe harbor, so what are we to make of Christ sending Simon to the deep or calling him out of the boat into the storm? What a mystery that Christ sends disciples where death and life teeter on the brink in the depths! Why doesn't Christ shelter us from inner storms? Is it possible that we are not sheltered because by plunging into the stormy waters, we find refuge, and that by diving into the deep, we discover safe haven?

Life seems to offer numerous opportunities to fathom our depths and admit sinfulness. For much of my life I've found it so much more gratifying to preach or teach about this than to practice it. Observing, critiquing, counseling, or just watching TV is easier than taking Christ's call to conversion and purification to heart. At this point in my life, I am catching glimpses as to how the path to admitting sinfulness involves clearly articulating the wounds I've suffered. It is becoming more important to account for the wounds I've inflicted on others. Nose-diving into the deep hurts. (A fundamental aspect of discipleship involves grieving.)

To shift the metaphor a tad, as painful as it is to have my sinfulness revealed, so much do I believe Christ will not only embrace the gnawing, pestilential rat inside one day, but will transform each of us into Love Outpoured. This story ends with me still rowing.

CHAPTER NINE

Liturgical Contemplative Practice

We should glory in the Cross of our Lord Jesus Christ,
in whom is our salvation, life, and resurrection;
through whom we are saved and delivered.

(Entrance Antiphon,
Evening Mass of the Lord's Supper;
see Galatians 6:14)

Renewed theological insight into the Paschal Mystery shapes our encounter with the Risen Christ and reveals the role that the intellect plays in being really present at liturgy. As I picture it, the mind (memory and understanding) matures in its knowledge of Christ through study. It enlists the will to embrace hungers, thirsts, and resistances in an enclosure, not a prison, dealing with them like a "horse whisperer," not a warden. The will forges a spiritual crucible to hold firmly yet gently whatsoever obstreperous feelings arise or whichever unruly passions surface in our engagements with Word or liturgical gesture. This method of Liturgical Contemplative Practice brings together the disciple's mind, will, and heart to encounter Christ anew.

Liturgical Contemplative Practice utilizes exercises of study and prayer performed alone or with others and apart from liturgy for the sake of returning afresh to liturgical engagement. Again, Liturgical Contemplative Practice invites worshippers to open one's interior vessel (will) to commingle a renewed theological grasp of liturgical Word and gesture (mind) with real emotional responses in a contemplative encounter with the Risen Christ.

Liturgical Contemplative Practice: Part I

Liturgical Contemplative Practice takes place apart from liturgy; it can be done alone or with a group. The first step is to begin with a theological study of a gesture or Scripture passage. It's important to note that study is different than contemplation. A theological investigation sketches a profile of the Christ we meet in prayer, asking, "who is this Jesus whom we encounter today."

The solid theological spadework I propose separates the chaff (preconceptions) from the wheat; it prunes away the tangled growth of what we knew or thought we knew previously (unidentified assumptions) to encourage a new and sturdier growth of faith. Here we embrace new dimensions of vulnerability as our previous notions are challenged. We choose risk over security by continually submitting to the discipline of study to purify and reinvigorate our understanding of the Triune God. After studying, we are able to return to encounter the Risen Christ anew through conscious liturgical participation.

Theological Study: Holy Thursday as Entrance into the Paschal Mystery

We will study, in its context, the foot washing that takes place during the Evening Mass of the Lord's Supper. This liturgy of the Evening Mass of the Lord's Supper is a deceptively simple celebration during which many of the Church's great theological themes are sounded. *The Roman Missal* states:

> After the proclamation of the Gospel, the Priest gives a homily in which light is shed on the principal mysteries that are commemorated in this Mass, namely, the Institution of the Holy Eucharist and of the priestly Order, and the commandment of the Lord concerning fraternal charity.

(Evening Mass of the Lord's Supper, 9)

Try preaching adequately on just those topics in ten or twelve minutes. These themes merge with Holy Thursday's opening the celebration of the Sacred Paschal Triduum and drawing the faithful into an intense encounter with the Paschal Mystery. Consider the liturgy's Entrance Antiphon: "We should glory in the Cross of our Lord Jesus Christ, / in whom is our salvation, life and resurrection. . . ." The antiphon articulates the centrality of the Paschal Mystery as yet another foundational element to be addressed in preaching, praying, and singing.

But, wait, there's more! Other prominent gestures on Holy Thursday rightly claim our attention: oils consecrated at the diocesan Chrism Mass that may be received before the liturgy;

the First Reading recalls the celebration of Passover, thus associating the Church with our ancestors in faith; and the Gloria reappears. The foot washing rightly draws considerable focus. The transfer of the Eucharist directs worshippers' attention toward Good Friday, while the empty tabernacle stands in silent witness. Holy Thursday sets a splendid table indeed.

For more than forty years, my ministry as liturgist, presider, and musician has convinced me that Holy Thursday is better understood as the Church's solemn entrance into the Sacred Paschal Triduum, that vast and exceedingly dense celebration of the Paschal Mystery that extends through Easter Vespers. The memorial of the Paschal Mystery, serving as the unifying focus for Triduum, centers worshippers on the kenotic Christ with each rite during the Three Days. So, let's consider the adequacy of the realization of foot washing.

Contemporary Implementation of Foot Washing Revisited

If therefore I, the Lord and Teacher, have washed your feet, you also ought to wash the feet of one another. I gave you (this) for an example in order that as I did to you, you also may do.

(John 13:13–15; my translation)

It has become conventional for homilists and liturgists to note that service is the indisputable meaning of the foot washing. Certainly, the Church's documents support this view:

> The washing of the feet of chosen [men] which, according to tradition, is performed on this day, represents the service and charity of Christ, who came "not to be served but to serve" (Matthew 20:28). This tradition should be maintained and its proper significance explained.[14]

Through homily, song, and the enactment of the rite, the washing of the feet is interpreted as service. One parish adheres to the practice of the priest-celebrant washing the feet of twelve males.[15] Another selects a variety of parishioners to represent the diversity of its congregation (gender, age, ethnic communities, etc.). A third parish invites members of the congregation to come to a chair to have their feet washed. Each would claim to interpret the Gospel mandate faithfully.

Yet, I've questioned whether service is the only way to understand the rite. I wonder whether such a strong emphasis on service protects disciples-in-training from encounters with personal vulnerability. This has led me to recommend that we reconceive the basic meaning of the foot washing. What if we considered it as an action aimed at sending disciples-in-training into our vulnerable depths *by being served*? Were this approach to prove satisfactory and fruitful, it would achieve several worthy goals: It would highlight the way we receive Christ's gift of salvation as well as uncover personal vulnerabilities we've been tempted to ignore by turning our conceptions on their heads. (The strong help the weak. I serve; therefore, I am not weak.) Finally, it would respect the potential of the rite to drive us to the depths of our being, and once there, to become really present to the Risen Christ. I propose, then, that disciples-in-training should relate first to Simon Peter as the model recipient of this ritual action. Rather than identifying with Christ only (a position of some power) we choose to interact with Outpouring Love from a position of vulnerability.

The Scriptural Context for the Liturgical Gesture of Foot Washing

A comprehensive study of the washing of feet would deal with the totality of its liturgical context by examining every spoken text and every gesture or symbol during the Holy Thursday liturgy. Unable to mount such an extensive analysis now, let us attend to Simon Peter and how he deals with his vulnerability.

Now before the feast of the Passover (*pascha*), Jesus knowing that his hour had come that he should depart out of this world to the Father, loving his own in the world, he loved them to the end (*eis telos*). And during the course of the supper, the devil had now put (it) into the heart of Judas, son of Simon, that he should hand him over. (And) knowing that the Father gave all things to him into his hands, and that he came forth from God and goes to God, he rose from the supper and placed aside his garments. And taking a towel, he girded himself. Then he put water in to the basin and began to wash the feet of the disciples and to wipe them with a towel with which he had been girded. He came therefore to Simon Peter; he said to him, "Lord, are you going to wash my feet?" And Jesus answered and said to him, "What I am doing, you do not know yet, but you will after these things." Peter said to him, "By no means shall you wash my feet even to the (end of the) age!" Jesus answered him, "Unless I wash you, you have no part with me." Simon Peter said to him, "Lord, not only my feet, but also the hands and head." Jesus said to him, "The one having been bathed has no need except to wash the feet, but is clean totally. And you are clean, but not all." He knew the one handing him over; therefore he said, "You are not all clean."

When therefore he washed their feet and took his garments (off) and reclined again, he said to them, "Do you know what I have done to you? You call me 'The Teacher' and 'The Lord' and well you say (this) for I am. If therefore I, the Lord and Teacher, have washed your feet, you also ought to wash the feet of one another. I gave you (this) for an example in order that as I did to you, you also may do."

(John 13:1–15; my translation)

It is absolutely crucial to recognize how, from the start, this passage links the foot washing to Jesus' Death on the Cross (18:1 — 19:42, Good Friday's Passion narrative) through specific vocabulary selections. We will look at those selections.

The hour: Jesus knew his hour had come, the hour in which he would glorify God by dying on the Cross. In John 2:4, 7:30, and 8:20, Jesus stated that his hour had not yet come. As the time drew close to his Passion, Jesus was aware that the time had arrived. "The hour has come for the Son of Man to be glorified," he states in 12:23 and "It is for this reason I have come to this hour. Father, glorify your name" in 12:27. He describes the hour, stating, "'And I, when I am lifted up from the earth, will draw all people to myself.' He said this indicating the kind of death he would die" (12:32–33).

To the end: John records that Jesus loved them "to the end." This creates an inclusion, a bookend, with his last words on the

Cross, "It is finished" (19:30). In both instances, the Gospel writer employs the noun, *telos*, or the Greek verb, *teleō*.

The Passover: John meticulously observes Jesus' relation to the Passover throughout the entire Gospel, underscoring it yet again in chapter 13 ("before the feast of the Passover"). In the Fourth Gospel, Jesus, the Lamb of God, dies on the Day of Preparation, before the Passover when the lambs were slaughtered (19:14).

Handing him over: John associates Jesus' gesture of washing feet with that moment in his Eucharistic discourse in chapter 6 when some disciples elected to follow him. In both instances, John refers to Judas' betrayal, literally, his "handing him over" (see John 6:64, 71). All is accomplished at the Cross.

These things: The refrain, "these things," appears here and in the Passion narrative in 19:36 and 38, where it specifically refers to Jesus' Death and the lancing of his side. The meaning of the foot washing will become known to Peter after Jesus' Death and Resurrection: "What I am doing, you do not know yet, but you will after these things."

The connections are decisive. First, John reveals how Love Outpoured in the foot washing is the very same love shown in his Death on the Cross ("to the end"). Second, John explicitly links receiving Jesus' ministry of foot washing with receiving Jesus' Death on the Cross: "Unless I wash you, you will have no part with me." Understanding the Cross, then, informs our grasp of the foot washing and vice versa. Behold what God has done for us! Third, John's portrayal of Jesus diverges from that displayed in the synoptic accounts of the Gospel or mainstream piety. The Fourth Gospel depicts Jesus as the Risen and Triumphant One who reveals God's glorious victory on the Cross. Matthew, Mark, and Luke, on the other hand, paint a more grief-stricken, humiliated, and anguished Jesus suffering at the hands of his tormenters. He's silent, like a sheep before its shearers. This is hardly so in John!

John portrays Jesus as in command of events throughout the Passion. When the soldiers and Pharisees come for him at night, Jesus announces the divine name, "I AM." During questioning, Jesus forcefully engages Annas, Caiphas, Pilate, and the soldier who slapped him; he's definitely not silent. When brought for judgment, it is Jesus, not Pilate, who sits on the judgment bench robed in royal purple. (The Greek is ambiguous here.) Jesus reigns from the Cross (INRI); he provides for his mother. Finally, when he dies, he hands over the Spirit. Jesus acts deliberately on our behalf, bold before his persecutors. This is the same Jesus who washes feet. The Word proclaimed sets us in relationship to this Jesus, our longstanding devotional attitudes notwithstanding. It is this Jesus who knows it is his hour; the Victor who dares intrude on our space, kneeling with water and towel.

Solid biblical and theological study such as what we have just done prunes what we knew or thought we knew to encourage a new and sturdier growth of faith. The challenge appears after the pruning, when we realize the loss of whatever perception of Jesus we previously relied upon. We've begun a long journey to maturity.

The Human Reception of Mystery:
Liturgical Contemplative Practice II

> I might remark in passing that what distinguishes a religious
> understanding from a merely intellectual one is that the former
> is not merely an understanding of the teaching of Jesus or its
> development by others, but an understanding of oneself and one's
> own experience in light of that.

(John Macmurray)[16]

Our first step in Liturgical Contemplative Practice Scripture study quickened our theological appreciation of Jesus Christ as proclaimed by John's Gospel account on Holy Thursday. In the chapter "The Maturity of Religion I" in *Reason and Emotion*, John Macmurray rightly refers to the results of such inquiry as intellectual rather than religious. He recognizes it as necessary yet not sufficient because it does not make our felt experience available for encounter with the Risen One *as we are*. Therefore, as our perception of the theological breadth of the Paschal Mystery develops, we simultaneously need to deepen our capacity for conscious, that is, affective, participation in the encounter.[17]

To accomplish this, the second component of Liturgical Contemplative Practice instructs disciples-in-training to assemble data from personal, affective responses to Word or gesture without judgment. This is the proper work of the cartographer-disciple who reconnoiters interior landscape dispassionately, locating where to welcome grace. Let us see how this second of three parts contributes to our encounter with Christ in the foot washing.

As the study session closes, the practitioner shifts into a more reflective mode. This can be done in a number of ways: focusing on breathing, relaxing and attending to Christ's presence, and any of the practices of the Church's contemplative tradition.

After a period of silence, the Gospel passage is read again meditatively. Then the words or phrases that stand out from the reading are noted, or the telling features of the gesture or symbol observed. At this time, we may ask whether the words, gestures, or symbols bring about images to our religious imagination and take in how we respond emotionally.

A gesture such as foot washing has the power to elicit intense reactions. What do you say to Jesus who kneels to wash your feet? The following are uncensored responses that have been shared with me:

- "Please don't wash my feet, Jesus! I'm so embarrassed. They stink! They're crooked! I don't want anyone to see them, much less touch them. I'm mortified. I'm afraid that their smell will offend you and drive you away."

- "Don't do me any favors, Jesus. I'm not helpless. I feel week and humiliated. I can take care of my own feet, thank you very much."

- "Please back off, Jesus. I feel uncomfortable when anyone kneels before me. I don't deserve to be served; I'm not good enough. I'm so ashamed. Please just leave; don't bother with me. "

- "I don't like anyone getting that close to me or touching me. Don't invade my space, Jesus! Don't touch me. Just stay away!"

- "No, please don't even look at me. I don't want to be in the spotlight. I don't want to be seen. Everyone can see me. They won't like what you see. Don't look at me!"

- "Don't touch me! There's something vaguely sexual about all this. I'm not sure what it is, but I don't like anyone touching my feet."

- "I don't want anyone to serve me. Let me serve you instead. I'm good at that. You sit right here."

- "How about this, Jesus, you wash my feet and I'll wash yours. Deal? That way I don't feel like I owe you anything."

Gathering Data for the Crucible of Contemplation: Naming Our Feelings

The next part of the exercise involves translating our immediate reactions into statements of feeling (marked in the examples below by italics) to locate ourselves precisely on the map of our spiritual lives. Noting resistances without evaluation is also key to ensuring our map is unsullied by deceptive judgments. This will lessen the chance of indulging in shame, which always misleads. Instead, reactions map the inner landscape in the presence of Christ.

- "Jesus, I'm afraid my smelly, ugly feet will offend you. You'll just abandon me in disgust like everyone else. I can't trust you" (desert of abandonment).

- "Don't look at me like I am helpless, Jesus. I can manage on my own, see! I'm terrified of being seen as weak or dependent" (wastelands of isolated self-sufficiency).

- "Don't get too close to me, Jesus. I'm not worthy. I hate the way I feel insignificant and inferior around everyone. I'm just no good. Please back off" (hidden fissures of inferiority).

- "Do not touch me. I fear you're trying to control me, to invade my space, to take over. Get back!" (frozen tundra of defensive self-protection).

- "Don't look at me! I have so many faults. I've been trying to be a better person. . . . Really. Just wait. You'll see some day. It just hurts when you look at me. I'm so ashamed" (forests of concealment; bog of shame).

- "Don't touch me! It brings up bad memories. I just don't know how to handle intimacy or to deal with these feelings. Do not lay a hand on me!" (Grand Canyon of painful experiences).

- "Don't serve me. I am the one who helps everyone else. That's my role. Don't take that from me or I'll feel dependent. I don't need your service" (the chilly Arctic of pride).

- "Let's make a deal, Jesus. I'll let you wash my feet if I can wash yours. I'm *mortified* at feeling *vulnerable*. I don't like feeling in debt to others. We can work this out!" (the foggy river-bottom of bargaining).

Do you identify with any of these reactions? Were you able to observe and record your reactions factually, without disapproval? A capacity to notice, welcome, and name the disruptive emotions that materialize is fundamental to the work of Liturgical Contemplative Practice as it guarantees the accuracy of the map of our interior lives. Through such work, we are able to say, "Here I am, Lord! Here's the place I guard. Here are the places I avoid." Naming our reactions clearly helps us pinpoint the particular place where we can welcome a more profound engagement with the Risen Christ.

The beauty of Liturgical Contemplative Practice, in the final analysis, is that it situates us directly in relationship to Jesus as teacher and Savior. It allows us to ask, "How willing am I to meet Christ in my vulnerability? To be taught?"

Liturgical Contemplative Practice also locates us before Christ as companions on a journey to maturation. First, we discover we are not alone in our struggles. We are all sinners, and all of us struggle. Second, study sessions promote experiences of solidarity, which in turn may support a more authentic, common prayer of the assembly. Third, study sessions could promote discernment of collective patterns of resistance to God's will, which may lead to communal repentance and conversion.

Encountering Christ in the Crucible: Part III

> One day, while crossing the Umbrian plain on horseback, [St.] Francis unexpectedly drew near a poor leper. The sudden appearance of this repulsive object filled him with disgust and he instinctively retreated, but presently controlling his natural aversion he dismounted, embraced the unfortunate man, and gave him all the money he had.[18]

The data gathered readies us to engage the Risen Christ as we are. In the concluding portion of the Liturgical Contemplative Practice session, then, a period of contemplation is entered. Participants already may be comfortable with a particular method. For example, contemplation may be a prayerful encounter that surrenders images of God (such as in the writings of Teresa of Avila, John of the Cross, and Thomas Keating). Others make active use of all five of the senses in their contemplation (as in the writing of St. Ignatius of Loyola). However, during Liturgical Contemplative Practice, participants are asked to imagine a "crucible" strong enough to contain powerful interactions. Its use here allows a vessel safely to hold our emotions and reactions. At this point, these steps are followed:

1. Prepare: A shift is made from studying and recording personal reactions to a prayerful, Christ-centered focus. For example, the individual might say: "I prepare my inner, spiritual crucible to welcome the Christ who kneels before me."

2. Create: In Liturgical Contemplative Practice, the will fashions in our religious imaginations a vessel that I like to call a crucible because of the intense interactions it contains. Into the crucible, participants pour deep emotional reactions to engagement with Christ in liturgical Word or gesture. At first, emotional reactions may feel too intense to hold. Yet, with practice, one's crucible can grow sturdier and more flexible.

3. Enter: We enter the crucible we have fashioned in our religious imaginations. We bring our whole selves.

4. Welcome: We welcome Christ into our crucible with the faith-filled knowledge gained from study. In the case of the passage we just worked with, we encounter the Jesus of John's Gospel account kneeling at our feet. Indeed, it is Love Outpoured whom we welcome. It is the Paschal Mystery we meet, who intrudes upon our comfort zones, calling us to an unknown future.

5. Ignite: Participants now pour into the crucible their passionate reactions to the foot washing. These secret storms deliver the fuel to fire whichever interactions need to occur between Christ and ourselves.

Contemplative prayer takes place in the vessel as engagement between two persons. We saw earlier, for example, how resistance to Jesus' washing our feet may develop from certain fears. Disciples-in-training learn to be present to Christ while yet fearful. They breathe into these emotions, thereby maintaining their real presence to Love Outpoured. The crucible supports this purifying encounter of embracing and being embraced by Christ.

6. Contemplate: Thus, participants give themselves permission to feel the hunger, thirst, resistance, resentment, or whichever emotion had been identified. The emotion(s) should be allowed to animate the interaction. Feeling statements can serve as a way to fan the flames, for example: "Jesus, I resist / hide from / fear you when you kneel to wash my feet. I welcome you here."

Similar to the practice of centering prayer, repetition of a sacred word supports the intention to stay emotionally present to Christ whenever distracted. The following are examples of sacred words or phrases that could be used: "Here I am," "You . . . with me," "Meet me, Lord," or simply, "Welcome." Unlike centering prayer, Liturgical Contemplative Practice encourages the practitioner to remain with the emotional reactions surfaced earlier (Liturgical Contemplative Practice II). The individual breathes in, holding the feeling in the gut, and repeats the "sacred word" on the out breath. Notice that as embracing meets being embraced *with the breath,* the work of contemplation transpires.

As much as possible now, the vulnerable self should be allowed to be embraced by the Risen Christ. The individual should be really present as she or he is to Christ, without demanding particular outcomes. Pause.

7. Converse: Participants now take a few moments to speak directly with Christ in their own words.

The words of Sts. Francis of Assisi and Ignatius of Loyola speak for many saints who grasped the significance of gratitude as the cornerstone of discipleship. Francis entreated, "Make me an instrument of your peace." Ignatius prayed, "Take, Lord, receive all my liberty." Our clear and sincere response is the key. It doesn't matter whether we reply to Christ from attraction or aversion. Why?

Transformation relies primarily on the graciousness of Outpouring Love. And, since grace builds on the ability to be vulnerable to ourselves and to the kenotic Christ, transformation relates to developing the capacity to be engaged by Love Outpoured as we are. Conversion results from our willingness to be embraced as hungry, thirsty, and resistant friends by Jesus Christ, who kneels in love to wash our feet.

8. Conclude: Conclude with the Lord's Prayer or another prayer.

9. Chronicle: Take time to record personal experiences in a journal or walk alone in preparation for meeting with a spiritual director, counselor, or sponsor. This practice also can be done before Mass as a way of immediately bringing these experiences of prayer into liturgy.

Liturgical Contemplative Practice directs disciples-in-training to remain attentive to any ill-tempered feelings that emerge in contemplative encounters with Christ. Our part in prayer involves simply doing our best to engage and be engaged by the Risen Christ. Authentically personal responses position disciples-in-training before the Risen Christ with fewer pretenses. As we allow resistances to appear, we also welcome the Christ who is always present to embrace, touch, speak to, and deal with our reactivity, our fierce independence, our fearful avoidance. The ongoing nature of discipleship invites us . . .

- to accept God's love even while hiding from personal disorders;

- to trust Jesus' love even while experiencing the depths of sinfulness or sorrow;

- to welcome Jesus' friendship while keeping his offer of self-giving love at bay;

- to be addressed by the life-giving Word even as we reinforce our deafness, blindness, or willfulness;

- to seek God's love even while still unwilling to surrender.

These incongruities point to predicaments and struggles of all good religious people. They arise whenever any of us honestly accounts for our reactions to encounters with the Paschal Mystery at depth. We either acknowledge what we see about ourselves or opt for blind hypocrisy.

We can learn to bring our whole selves into relationship with this daunting yet compelling presence of Jesus, who kneels before us as we are and says, "Unless I wash you, you have no part with me, my friend." Situated here, we discover that Christ has already found us. Here it's possible to experience what it truly means to be a loved sinner, welcomed by Christ in our very act of resistance. It's no longer theory but a reality we experience.

CHAPTER 10

The Communion Procession: People in Need, People Who Receive

I can will what is right, but I cannot do it. For I do not do the good I want, but the evil I do not want is what I do. For I delight in the law of God, in my inmost self, but I see in my members another law at war with the law of my mind, making me captive to the law of sin that dwells in my members. Wretched man that I am! Who will rescue me from this body of death? Thanks be to God through Jesus Christ our Lord!

(Romans 7:18b–19, 22–24)

I hope my approach to mindfully preparing for and participating in liturgy are clearer now. To summarize, first, as we mature in faith, disciples-in-training grow in the capacity to observe and name our emotional responses to Word and liturgical gesture. Second, as we move out of concealment, we see ourselves with greater clarity and rather than recoiling instinctively, we become willing to welcome Christ, trusting that he welcomes us as we are. By taking account of our gut-driven reactions to the Word, we come to engage and be engaged by Love Outpoured as we truly are and not as we wish to be. Through this, I believe it is possible to integrate even the harshest feelings, attitudes, and experiences into our real presence to the Real Presence.

One of the personal reactions that conscious engagement with the Paschal Mystery elicits can be particularly crippling, so it's worth close attention. Some people believe that disciples must be absolutely pure, faultless, innocent, and unassailably perfect to enter the presence of God worthily. Whether by temperament or training, nature or nurture, countless disciples-in-training carry the burden of perfectionism. Assessments concerning being "good enough" before God and others can hinder us from a full experience of the Paschal Mystery.

Fortunately, a specific moment in the Liturgy of the Eucharist —the Communion procession—invites disciples-in-training to inhabit the tension between the human notion of perfection and the divine gift of wholeness.

It is beyond question that it is good to be good. It is virtuous to do good. When circumstances arise that inspire the noblest of responses, we take appropriate satisfaction in answering the call. Unconditional love is rightly seen as the highest of human qualities, recognizable in a host of generous responses. Still, no one is perfect. We are all sinful. Don't we default to self-preservation at times? How are we to handle, then, the discrepancy between intending to live out the highest of ideals while floundering in distressing self-interest?

Some persons turn irritation at the messes they have made into preemptive strikes as they criticize themselves. Others adopt a spirituality of *trying*, hoping to stave off divine retribution. Out of horror at failing and the dread of being seen as a mess, they say, "If God or anyone else saw me, I would be abandoned. I'm such a disaster! I'm trying; God knows that I'm trying. I just don't seem to get any better. If I can only change, I will merit love." Exasperation with personal weakness generates a vow to improve so as to fend off God's disapproving judgment. The problem stands that perfectionism's goal is elusive, an ever moving target.

The opposite of perfection is not necessarily laxity; it is trust. Trust orients disciples-in-training toward gracious acceptance of incompleteness bolstered by durable experiences of divine mercy. Disciples live in the tension between saint and sinner, between whole and incomplete, between the ideal and the real. And this tension reveals itself to us through conscious participation in liturgical prayer. The *Constitution on the Sacred Liturgy* states that the liturgy makes "the work of our redemption a present actuality" (2). Liturgy is about redemption, not condemnation. CSL states,

> From the liturgy, therefore, particularly the eucharist, grace is poured forth upon us as from a fountain; the liturgy is the source for achieving in the most effective way possible *human sanctification* and God's *glorification*, the end to which all the Church's other activities are directed.
>
> (10; emphases added)

Interesting. Liturgy sanctifies the Church. Also intriguing is the manner in which we are to come to the liturgy:

In order that the liturgy may possess its full effectiveness, *it is necessary that the faithful come to it with proper dispositions*, that their minds be attuned to their voices, and that they cooperate with divine grace, lest they receive it in vain.

(11; emphases added)

Does this explanation imply that worshippers are required to be spotless to attend liturgy? I don't believe so. Instead, I propose that "proper dispositions" have to do with bringing our whole sinful, resistant selves to encounter Christ in order to glorify God and be sanctified through liturgical participation. It has nothing to do with being perfect, with *not* being a sinner. We might worship without explicit sin, yet we are always sinners who will be made whole, perfect, and complete *only* at the Supper of the Lamb.

Let us observe, then, how the Communion procession reveals sinners advancing to receive a foretaste of and a share in the (eschatological) banquet, which will be fully realized only on the Last Day. Christ welcomes all the faithful on pilgrimage to the final banquet *today*. Setting aside instances of mortal sin, each person comes to God coping with compromised abilities to respond. Note that the very last prayer before the procession affirms that unworthiness does not prevent us from receiving Christ's healing presence. Echoing the centurion speaking to Jesus, we say: "Lord, I am not worthy that you should enter under my roof, but only say the word and my soul shall be healed." There is welcome at the table for sinners. There is room at the banquet for those among us who still need to strive to become good on our own terms. There is room for all of us to dine joyfully on Love Outpoured as sinners.

Hold in your mind's eye the Communion procession: persons of various ages, sizes, shapes, colors, and temperaments with varied gifts and challenges, joys and sorrows, burdens and victories all come to receive the Bread of Life. Freeze-frame! Notice how we implicitly yet publicly announce our status as sinners (along with those who flocked to dine with Jesus *then*, when he walked the earth) simply by joining this procession *now*. (See Mark 2:13–17; Matthew 9:9–13; Luke 5:27–32.) Meditate on this scene.

When we're aware of this meaning, simply joining this procession can evoke responses that help us locate where we need to welcome Christ. Individuals might say: "Don't think of me as a sinner, look at *those people*." "I'm just here to get fueled up for the week." "Yes, I do sin, but I'm not so bad." "I'm really trying to be better." "Don't look at me!" Many of us bargain when we are named sinners.

Next, continue the frame and notice people extending their hands to receive. Freeze-frame! Meditate on the hand, cupped and extended. Open your hand in front of you for several moments. Does it convey both need and receiving?

The cupped hand is an image of need: "More," said Dickens' Oliver. It is hard to admit our need. "I'm *never* hungry, Jesus. I work for my food." This gesture of open hands has the potential to call forth proper dispositions. "I fill my hungry self with so much stuff.

Please don't let me receive you as just another thing." "I'm ashamed of my emptiness, Jesus. Feed me! I can't do it myself." It situates disciples-in-training as hungry by employing the universal sign of need and drawing out the recognition that we cannot manufacture the Bread of Life ourselves.

So we stretch out our hands, hungering for so much: love, justice, acceptance, knowledge, money, meaning, security, wisdom, community, shelter, companionship, order, freedom, God, family, intimacy, world peace, relief from pain, health, friendship, happiness, relief, healing, or change. Can we consciously hold our hungry selves in our empty hands while proceeding to receive?

Open hands are also an image of receiving. With the frame still frozen, see Christ welcome the hungry to the paschal banquet. All who approach his table are fed. See starving people offered blessed food from his hand at this moment, no matter their capacity to respond. Christ offers life *today* as a foretaste of what he will share *then* at the final banquet. Jesus ate with sinners *then*. Christ still feeds hungry sinners *today*. What is it like to be fed with a tiny wafer—Christ the fullness of life—and still be hungry? Taste and see the goodness of the Lord! Taste the joy of being nourished!

Obviously, I've anticipated an inventory of personal reactions to processing with hands stretched forth. These images are like responses to the Word described earlier. This gesture lays "open to the eyes" some very tender and vulnerable areas. For example, open hands waiting to be fed can open the realm of personal and corporate avoidance of emptiness. Once again: "Hungry or empty? Not in the least. I take care of myself. I'm no beggar." Or, regarding the starving of the world: "Not my problem, Jesus. I provide for mine. They can do the same." Or, concerning our status as sinners: "I'm not so bad, Jesus. . . . Just a few faults . . ."

Our mindful encounter with the kenotic graciousness of Christ, embodied in hands outstretched in procession, has the potential to provoke significant reactions that arise from our deepest, and often undisclosed, hunger and need. Indeed, these surface almost effortlessly whenever we *consciously* receive the Bread of Life.

There's more. The human propensity to deny sinfulness and hunger points us toward a related arena of avoidance: the hunger and need of the world's poor and oppressed. To reckon with this, recall the Communion procession. Note how, in *Mane Nobiscum Domine* (MND), 28, Pope John Paul II challenges individualistic perspectives on the reception of Communion:

> There is one other point which I would like to emphasize, since it significantly affects the authenticity of our communal sharing in the Eucharist. It is the impulse which the Eucharist gives to the community *for a practical commitment to building a more just and fraternal society.* In the Eucharist our God has shown love in the extreme, overturning all those criteria of power which too often govern human relations and radically affirming the criterion of service: "If anyone would be first, he must be last of all and servant of all" (Mark 9:35). . . . Saint Paul vigorously reaffirms the impropriety of a Eucharistic celebration lacking charity expressed by practical sharing with the poor (cf. 1 Corinthians 11:17–22, 27–34).

Continuing in the same article in MND, the pope asks that parishes and dioceses commit to responding to poverty. In associating receiving Communion with working for a just world, the pope sets a lofty standard for judging the authenticity of our Eucharistic celebrations.

> I think for example of the tragedy of hunger which plagues hundreds of millions of human beings, the diseases which afflict developing countries, the loneliness of the elderly, the hardships faced by the unemployed, the struggles of immigrants. These are evils which are present—albeit to a different degree—even in areas of immense wealth. We cannot delude ourselves: by our mutual love and, in particular, by our concern for those in need we will be recognized as true followers of Christ (cf. John 13:35; Matthew 25:31–46). *This will be the criterion by which the authenticity of our Eucharistic celebrations is judged.*
>
> (emphases added)

That is indeed a magnanimous vision. So, how do you like these words of Pope John Paul II? Can hungry people share with others? Is hoarding our final recourse? How much food, how much stuff is enough to nourish our hungry hearts? How much can we give before insecurity and self-defensive clinging erupt? When disciples-in-training receive the Bread of Life, we self-identify as needy, poor, sinful persons. What would it take for us to respond generously to other needy, poor, and sinful persons on the planet? Finally, we need to ask ourselves if we can endure our hungers long enough to regard the hungry of the world with purposeful compassion?

We have reflected on what a conscious engagement between disciples-in-training and Christ's kenotic love might look like during the Communion procession. This returns us to a moment of discernment: Does God require childlike purity, blameless virtue, and unblemished innocence from us whenever we approach the banquet?

It seems to me that we have two options. One is to judge all feelings of resistance as negative. Quell all storms. Ignore them. Try harder. Bargain. Try again even harder. Lock down negative feelings. Live in fear. Keep trying! Or, we can admit resistance to God and welcome regular transforming encounters with Christ's person. As worshippers consciously accounting for the ways we receive the Paschal Mystery, we are able to meet Christ as we are and discover that our immersion into Outpouring Love happens explicitly for us as sinners, beloved and sent on mission.

Here is an image I hope serves as a workable metaphor for the Church's encounter with the Paschal Mystery in liturgy: When I was about ten years old, I caught a nasty cold. Mom threw together Grandma's famed mustard plaster. She mixed dry mustard with flour, added water, and whisked it into a paste. She spread this poultice onto an old cloth diaper and placed it on my back while I lay in bed. It was cold at first, but then it began to warm up slowly. Soon, the warmth became uncomfortably hot. This old-fashioned home remedy extracted all those ill humors and, along with medications, restored me to health. The liturgy, in my estimation, works similarly. Liturgical engagement with Divine Love creates a safe, loving context that draws all the negativity we avoid to the surface in the presence of the One whose welcome to the table ultimately heals us and makes us real. I have come to see that when we, as worshippers, bring our deep reactions and resistances into relationship with kenotic love and through that become more vulnerable, we manifest conscious, real presence to the Real Presence.

I invite you to meditate on a poem from the religious writings of Rabindranath Tagore, poet laureate of India during the early-to-mid-twentieth century. This poem from *Gitanjali* poignantly tells of the plight of a sinner whose deep desire for God clashes with his all-too-human patterns of defiance. Grace labors long as the singer embraces his resistance as part of the relationship while neither hiding from nor fleeing the divine presence. In truth, his desire for God is neither diminished nor diverted. Instead, the singer trusts Love to have the final word beyond storm and rebellion. To my mind, this poem expresses the hope of every disciple. It is a hope that is met every time we bring ourselves—our whole, flawed yet real and hopeful selves—to Christ in the liturgy.

> That I want thee, only thee—let my heart repeat without end.
> All the desires that distract me, day and night,
> are false and empty to the core.
> As the night keeps hidden in its gloom the petition for light,
> even thus in the depths of my unconscious rings the cry—
> I want thee, only thee.
> As the storm still seeks its end in peace
> when it strikes against peace with all its might,
> even thus my rebellion strikes against thy love
> and still its cry is—
> I want thee, only thee.

NOTES

1. Annibale Bugnini, *The Reform of the Liturgy, 1948–1975*, trans. Matthew J. O'Connell (Collegeville: The Order of St. Benedict, 1990), 39.

2. I am grateful to Joyce Ann Zimmerman, CPPS, editor of *Liturgical Ministry* magazine, for the opportunity to edit my previously published article. See Roc O'Connor, SJ, "The Threat of the Paschal Mystery," in *Liturgical Ministry* 12 (Winter 2003): 52–56. It appeared in *Liturgical Ministry* in a series of columns illustrating Zimmerman's conviction that the Church needs to come to a more profound knowledge of and encounter with the Paschal Mystery in contemporary worship.

3. Robert E. Taft, SJ, "What Does Liturgy Do? Toward a Soteriology of Liturgical Celebration: Some Theses," in *Beyond East and West: Problems in Liturgical Understanding*, 2nd rev. and enlarged ed., (Rome: Edizioni Orientalia Christiana [Pontifical Oriental Institute], 1997), 244 (emphasis mine). I am indebted to Fr. Taft's insights, which I rely upon throughout this section.

4. I wish to thank Fr. Peter Fink, SJ, for this insight.

5. Foreword by Edward J. Kilmartin, SJ, in Jean Corbon, *The Wellspring of Worship*, trans. Matthew J. O'Connell, (New York: Paulist Press, 1988), v.

6. Cf. *Summa Theologiae*, 1a, q. 75, a. 5; 3a, q. 5.

7. These are my translations of the Scripture passages.

8. Mark Searle, "Journey of Conversion," *Worship* 54 (January, 1980): 52 (emphases added).

9. Alexander Schmemann, chapter 4 "Liturgy and Theology," chap. 4 in *Liturgy and Tradition: Theological Reflections of Alexander*

Schmemann, ed. Thomas Fisch (Crestwood, NY: St. Vladimir's Seminary Press, 1990), 51–52. This chapter was taken from Alexander Schmemann, "Liturgy and Theology," *The Greek Orthodox Theological Review*, 17 (1972): 86–100

10. Ronald Rolheiser, *The Restless Heart: Finding Our Spiritual Home in Times of Loneliness* (New York: Image Books/Doubleday, 2006), 42.

11. Bishop Berkeley, "Of the Principles of Human Knowledge," pt. 1, no. 3 of *A Treatise Concerning the Principles of Knowledge*, (1710). Bishop Berkeley's idealist philosophy maintained the nonexistence of material objects in order to uphold common sense and to deny a foothold to atheism: "But sensible objects are nothing more than collections of sensible qualities, so they are merely complex ideas in the minds of those who perceive them. For such ideas, Berkeley held, to be just is to be perceived (in Latin, *esse est percipi*). There is no need to refer to the supposition of anything existing outside our minds, which could never be shown to resemble our ideas, since 'nothing can be like an idea but an idea.' Hence, there are no material objects." See *Philosophy Pages* at http://www.philosophypages.com/hy/4r.htm#intro.

12. With gratitude to Dr. Wendy Wright for her permission, I edited a section of our jointly published article. I put her insights to good use for this section of the chapter. See Roc O'Connor, SJ, and Wendy M. Wright, "'Just As I Am': A Spirituality for Disciples," in *Pastoral Music* 28:2 (December–January 2004): 35–40. Used with permission. See pages 12–14.

13. "The end of this Society is to devote itself with God's grace not only to the salvation and perfection of its members own souls, *but also with that same grace to labor strenuously in giving aid toward the salvation and perfection of the souls of their neighbors*" (emphases added). See "The First and General Examen Which Should Be Proposed to All Who Ask for Admission into the Society of Jesus: Chapter 1 — The Institute of the Society of Jesus and the Diversity of Its Members, 3,"

The Constitutions of the Society of Jesus and Their Complementary Norms, (St. Louis: The Institute of Jesuit Sources, 1996), 24.

14. Congregation for Divine Worship, *Circular Letter Concerning the Preparation and Celebration of the Easter Feasts*, "IV: Holy Thursday Evening Mass of the Lord's Supper," 51.

15. *The Roman Missal* indicates that the Washing of Feet is optional, "where a pastoral reason suggests it." It is not required that the feet of twelve people be washed. Rather, the Missal states, "The men who have been chosen are led by the ministers to seats prepared in a suitable place. Then the Priest (removing his chasuble if necessary) goes to each one, and, with the help of the ministers, pours water over each one's feet and dries them" (10–12).

16. John Macmurray, "The Maturity of Religion I," in *Reason and Emotion*, (Atlantic Highlands, New Jersey: Humanities Press International, Inc., 1992), 147.

17. Kathleen Hughes, *Saying Amen: A Mystagogy of Sacrament*, (Chicago: Liturgy Training Publications, 1999), especially pp. 1–32. Hughes articulates three criteria for active participation: first, awareness that liturgy is God's action; second, paying attention to the action of liturgical prayer as it unfolds; third, attunement to one's state of heart and soul.

18. P. Robinson, "St. Francis of Assisi," in *The Catholic Encyclopedia* (New York: Robert Appleton Company) accessed May 1, 2011, http://www.newadvent.org/cathen/06221a.htm.